£4

PENGUIN BOOKS

FREGE

Sir Anthony Kenny is Warden of Rhodes House, Oxford, and a Professorial Fellow of St John's College, Oxford. From 1964 to 1978 he was Fellow and Tutor in Philosophy at Balliol College, and was Master of that College from 1978 to 1989. His many published works include *Action, Emotion and Will* (1963), *Descartes* (1968), *Wittgenstein* (1973), *Will, Freedom and Power* (1975), *The Aristotelian Ethics* (1978), *Freewill and Responsibility* (1978), *Aristotle's Theory of the Will* (1979), *The Legacy of Wittgenstein* (1984), *The Metaphysics of Mind* (1989), *Aristotle on the Perfect Life* (1992) and *Aquinas on Mind* (1993). Most recently he has edited *The Oxford Illustrated History of Western Philosophy* (1994). He has been visiting professor at a number of universities in North America and holds nine honorary doctorates from universities in Britain, Ireland and the United States. Elected a Fellow of the British Academy in 1974 he served as President for the period 1989–93. He is currently Chairman of the British Library Board.

D1331225

ANTHONY KENNY

FREGE

PENGUIN BOOKS

PENGUIN BOOKS

Published by the Penguin Group
Penguin Books Ltd, 27 Wrights Lane, London W8 5TZ, England
Penguin Books USA Inc., 375 Hudson Street, New York, New York 10014, USA
Penguin Books Australia Ltd, Ringwood, Victoria, Australia
Penguin Books Canada Ltd, 10 Alcorn Avenue, Toronto, Ontario, Canada M4V 3B2
Penguin Books (NZ) Ltd, 182–190 Wairau Road, Auckland 10, New Zealand

Penguin Books Ltd, Registered Offices: Harmondsworth, Middlesex, England

First published 1995
3 5 7 9 10 8 6 4 2

Printed in England by Clays Ltd, St Ives plc

CONTENTS

PREFACE

Twenty years ago I published an introductory Penguin book on Wittgenstein. It sold widely, and Penguin Books commissioned me to write a similar introduction to Frege for the general reader. However, in the same year, 1973, there appeared the first massive volume of Michael Dummett's magisterial study of Frege, *Frege, Philosophy of Language* (London, Duckworth, 1973). It would have been premature to publish a popular work on Frege while Dummett's authoritative interpretation was still incomplete. Accordingly, it was agreed that I should postpone writing the book until Dummett's second volume appeared. This, in the event, was not until 1991.

In the meantime, Dummett has placed the learned world in his debt by a whole number of intermediary works. *The Interpretation of Frege's Philosophy* appeared in 1981 (London, Duckworth) and *Frege and Other Philosophers* appeared in 1991 (Oxford University Press). Also in 1991 appeared the book that had originally been planned as the second volume of a two-volume work, *Frege, Philosophy of Mathematics* (London, Duckworth).

When Dummett's final volume appeared I began to write the present work. His influence on me, as on any other writer on Frege, has been enormous, and has probably affected every page. I have not, however, signalled my debts to him in detail, nor have I drawn attention to the rare places where, after some hesitation, I have ventured to disagree with his interpretation. In general, I have tried to write in such a way that the reader does not need to get involved in evaluating contemporary interpretations of Frege, whether those of Dummett or of any other writer. I have tried to avoid controversial issues where possible, and when I have had to take sides I have done so silently.

Dummett addresses himself to a readership familiar with contemporary logic and philosophy. This book is directed primarily at the general reader who may be ignorant of both, and I have tried not to assume technical knowledge of any kind. I believe, in fact, that a reading of Frege is one of the best ways of finding one's way into modern analytic philosophy. Frege gave philosophy its current linguistic turn, yet his work addresses philosophical issues which are so clearly fundamental that no scope is given to the prejudices of those who believe that if philosophy is linguistic it must be trivial.

The chapters of the book are not organized by subject matter, but follow Frege's thought in chronological sequence. This involves some repetition, as philosophical topics recur several times. However, the purpose of the book is to assist a reader to work through Frege's own writings, and for this purpose a chronological ordering is probably the most helpful.

Anthony Kenny, Michaelmas 1993

ACKNOWLEDGEMENTS

I am grateful to Basil Blackwell, Publisher, for permission to quote passages from J. L. Austin's translation *The Foundations of Arithmetic* and from the translations by various hands in Frege's *Collected Papers on Mathematics, Logic and Philosophy*, ed. B. McGuinness.

I am deeply indebted to Peter Geach, who read the whole book in typescript and drew my attention to serious errors, which I have done my best to expunge from the final version.

Anthony Kenny

ABBREVIATIONS IN REFERENCES
TO WORKS OF FREGE

References have been given not to the German editions of Frege, but to the most widely available English versions. These are listed below in the order of the publication of the German originals.

CN   *Conceptual Notation and Related Articles.* Translated and edited with a biography and introduction by Terrell Ward Bynum. Oxford University Press, 1972.

FA   *The Foundations of Arithmetic: A logico-mathematical inquiry into the concept of number.* English translation by J. L. Austin. Oxford, Blackwell, 1950, 1953, 1980.

CP   *Collected Papers on Mathematics, Logic and Philosophy.* Edited by Brian McGuinness, translated by Max Black, V. H. Dudman, Peter Geach, Hans Kaal, E-H. W. Kluge, Brian McGuinness and R. H. Stoothoff. Oxford, Blackwell, 1984. This superseded the 1952 collection of translations from Frege edited by Peter Geach and Max Black cited below. Some features of the earlier translations are preferable, and the earlier volume is much freer from misprints.

BLA   *The Basic Laws of Arithmetic: Exposition of the system.* Translated and edited, with an introduction, by Montgomery Furth. University of California Press, Berkeley, 1964. This contains a translation of the first volume of Frege's *Grundgesetze der Arithmetik*, and of the appendix to the second volume.

GB *Translations from the Philosophical Writings of Gottlob Frege*. Edited and translated by Peter Geach and Max Black. Oxford, Blackwell, 1952, 1960. This contains translations of sections 56–67, 86–137 and 139–147 of *Grundgesetze der Arithmetik*.

PW *Posthumous Writings*. Edited by Hans Hermes, Friedrich Kambartel and Friedrich Kaulbach, translated by Peter Long and Roger White, Oxford, Blackwell, 1979.

PMC *Philosophical and Mathematical Correspondence*. Abridged for the English edition by Brian McGuinness and translated by Hans Kaal. Oxford, Blackwell, 1979.

CHAPTER 1

BIOGRAPHICAL INTRODUCTION
TO FREGE'S PHILOSOPHY

Gottlob Frege was a nineteenth-century German university professor, little known in his own lifetime, who devoted himself to thinking, teaching and writing. He played no part in public affairs, and much of his life was spent in the classroom and in the library. His books and articles were read by very few of his colleagues, and for a long time, even after his death, his influence in philosophy was exercised mainly through the writings of others. Today he is revered as the founder of modern mathematical logic, and as a philosopher of logic in the same rank as Aristotle. As a philosopher of mathematics he stands out, in the history of the subject, beyond all others.

Frege was born of a Lutheran family in Wismar, on the Baltic coast of Germany, in 1848. His father was the founder of a girls' school. Before Frege graduated from high school, in 1866, his father died. During his education and early academic career, he depended for financial support on his mother, who had succeeded her husband as principal of the girls' school.[1]

Frege entered Jena University in 1869 and spent four semesters there before moving to Göttingen in 1871 for five further semesters, studying philosophy, physics and mathematics. He submitted a dissertation on a geometrical topic and was awarded his Ph.D. by Göttingen in December 1873 (CP, 92).

---

1. For the details of this biography I have drawn on T.W. Bynum's introduction to CN.

1

Once the degree was granted, Frege applied for an unsalaried teaching post at Jena University. In support of his application he submitted a paper, 'Methods of Calculation based on an Extension of the Concept of Quantity' (CP, 56–92), which made a novel contribution to mathematical analysis. It was well received by the examiners, and Frege was appointed to the post in spite of the fact that his performance at the oral examination was reported to be 'neither quick-witted nor fluent'.

Frege began lecturing as a *privatdozent* in 1874 and he taught in the mathematics faculty at Jena for forty-four years. He was a clear, conscientious and demanding teacher, and for some years he had to carry the teaching load of a senior colleague who was an invalid. None the less, in the first five years after his appointment, he carried out research which was to lay the foundations of his life's work and which provided the starting point for an entirely new discipline.

Frege began his career as a mathematician at an exciting period in the history of mathematics. Euclidean geometry, which had been regarded as a system of necessary truths for over two millennia, lost its unique status early in the nineteenth century. Euclid had derived the theorems of his system from five axioms: it was now shown that one of these axioms, far from being a necessary truth, could be denied without inconsistency, and non-Euclidean geometries were developed on the basis of alternative axioms. There were also exciting developments in number theory. Imaginary numbers, such as $\sqrt{-1}$, which had been regarded as an eccentric curiosity in the eighteenth century, were shown to serve a purpose in the representation of motion in a plane, and were incorporated along with more familiar kinds of number in a general theory of complex numbers. The Dublin mathematician Sir William Hamilton devised a calculus of hyper-complex numbers (quaternions) to help in representing motion in a plane. At Halle in Germany Georg Cantor was working out, while Frege was a young professor, the theory of infinite numbers which he was to publish in 1883.

Frege early came to believe that the luxuriant expansion of

mathematics in his time was inadequately supported. This entire impressive construction, he claimed, rested on shaky foundations. Mathematicians did not really understand what they were about, even at the most basic level. The problem was not a lack of understanding of the true nature of imaginary numbers such as $\sqrt{-1}$, or of irrational numbers such as $\sqrt{2}$ or π, or of fractional numbers like $\frac{2}{3}$ or of negative integers such as -1; the lack of understanding began with the natural numbers such as 1, 2 and 3. Mathematicians, in Frege's view, could not explain the nature of the primary objects of their science or the fundamental basis of the discipline they taught. He resolved to devote his life to remedying this defect: setting out, in a perspicuous manner, the logical and philosophical foundations of arithmetic. A series of publications between his thirtieth and his sixtieth year was devoted to this end.

The first of these was a pamphlet issued in 1879 with the title *Begriffschrift*, which we can render into English as *Concept Script*. The concept script which gave the book its title was a new symbolism designed to bring out with clarity logical relationships which ordinary language concealed. The calculus contained in the book was a significant development in the history of logic.

For generations now the curriculum in formal logic has begun with the study of the propositional calculus. This is the branch of logic that deals with those inferences which depend on the force of negation, conjunction, disjunction, etc. when applied to sentences as wholes. Its fundamental principle is to treat the truth-value (that is, the truth or falsehood) of sentences which contain connectives such as 'and', 'if', 'or' as being determined solely by the truth-values of the component sentences which are linked by the connectives. Frege's *Concept Script* contains the first systematic formulation of the propositional calculus; it is presented in an axiomatic manner in which all laws of logic are derived, by a specified method of inference, from a number of primitive principles. Frege's symbolism, though elegant, is difficult to print, and is no longer used; but the operations which it expresses continue to be fundamental in mathematical logic.

Frege's greatest contribution to logic was his invention of quantification theory: a method of symbolizing and rigorously displaying those inferences that depend for their validity on expressions such as 'all' or 'some', 'any' or 'every', 'no' or 'none'. In *Concept Script*, using a novel notation for quantification, he presented an original calculus to formalize such inferences (a 'functional calculus' or 'predicate calculus' as it was later to be called). This laid the basis for all subsequent developments in logic and formalized the theory of inference in a more rigorous and more general way than the traditional Aristotelian syllogistic which up to the time of Kant was looked on as the be-all and end-all of logic.

In the *Concept Script* Frege was not interested in logic for its own sake. His aim was not simply to show how to conduct logic in a mathematical manner; he wanted to show that logic and mathematics were much more closely linked with each other than had previously been realized.

Before Frege addressed the subject, the nature of mathematics was the subject of debate between two schools of philosophical thought. According to Immanuel Kant (1724–1804) our knowledge of both arithmetic and geometry depends on intuition. His *Critique of Pure Reason* set out the position that mathematical truths were, in his terminology, both synthetic and a priori, which means that, while they were genuinely informative, they were known in advance of all experience. John Stuart Mill (1806–1873), on the other hand, thought mathematical truths were known a posteriori, that is to say, on the basis of experience. His *A System of Logic* argued the case that they were empirical generalizations widely applicable and widely confirmed.

The nature of mathematical truth had a central significance in philosophy. It was crucial to the question at issue between empiricist philosophers, who maintained that all our knowledge derived from sense experience, and rationalist philosophers, who maintained that the most universal and important elements of our knowledge derived from some supra-sensible source. Thus Mill says that his *System* 'met the intuition philosophers on ground on which they had previously been deemed unassailable; and it gave its own explanation, from experience and association, of that peculiar character of what are called necessary truths, which is adduced as proof that their evidence must come from a deeper source than experience'.[2]

Frege agreed with Kant against Mill that mathematics was known a priori. But he maintained that the truths of arithmetic were not synthetic at all; he denied that they contained any information not implicit in the nature of thought itself. Unlike geometry – which, he agreed with Kant, rested on a priori intuition – arithmetic was analytic; it was, indeed, nothing more than a branch of logic.

Frege's long-term purpose was to show that arithmetic could be formalized without the use of any non-logical notions or axioms, and that it was based solely upon general laws which were operative in every sphere of knowledge and needed no support from empirical facts. *Concept Script*, in addition to its formalization of propositional and functional calculus, contained some important preparatory work towards this reduction of arithmetic to logic; but the full presentation of Frege's thesis had to wait for the publication of his book *The Foundations of Arithmetic* in 1884.

On the basis, partly, of *Concept Script* Frege was promoted to a salaried professorship in 1879. The book, however, was not well received by the logical or mathematical world in general. Frege's notation was two-dimensional and tabular; this appeared to reviewers to be cumbersome and futile. Several writers compared the book unfavourably with George Boole's *An Investigation of the Laws of Thought*, which had appeared in 1854 and had regimented logic into formulas which resembled familiar arithmetical equations. Frege's publications between 1879 and 1884

2. J.S. Mill, *Autobiography*, Oxford University Press, 1971, p. 135.

consisted mainly of responses to hostile reviews and explanations of how his purposes and methods differed from those of Boole.

Perhaps because of the unfavourable reception of *Concept Script*, Frege wrote *The Foundations of Arithmetic* in a very different style. Symbols appear comparatively rarely, and there is a constant attempt to relate the discussion to the work of other writers. The thesis that arithmetic is derivable from logic – the thesis later to be known by the name of 'logicism' – is set out in this book fully and clearly, but for the most part quite informally.

Almost half the book is devoted to an attack on the ideas of Frege's predecessors and contemporaries, including Kant and Mill. In the course of these attacks the ground is prepared for the logicist position. In the main body of the work Frege showed how to replace the general arithmetical notion of number with logical notions such as the notion of a concept, the notion of an object's falling under a concept, the notion of equivalence between concepts and the notion of the extension of a concept. He offered definitions, in purely logical terms, of the numbers zero and one, and of the relation which each number has to its predecessor in the number series. From these elements, along with the general laws of logic, he offered to derive the whole of number theory.

The Foundations of Arithmetic is a very remarkable book; but when it appeared it received an even poorer reception than *Concept Script*. Only three reviews appeared, all of them hostile, and for almost twenty years the book went virtually unremarked. Frege was disappointed, but not deterred from further work on his great project.

In the *Foundations* there are two theses to which Frege attached great importance. The first is that each individual number is a self-subsistent object. The second is that the content of a statement assigning a number is an assertion about a concept, so that, for instance, the statement 'The Earth has one moon' assigns the number 1 to the concept *moon of the Earth.*

At first sight these theses may seem to conflict, but if we understand what Frege meant by 'concept' and 'object' we see that they are complementary. In saying that a number is an object, Frege is not suggesting that a number is something tangible like a tree or a table. Rather, he is doing two other things. First, he is denying that number is a property belonging to anything, whether to an individual or to a collection. Secondly, he is also denying that it is anything subjective, any mental item or any property of a mental item. Concepts are, for Frege, mind-independent, and so there is no contradiction between the thesis that numbers are objective, and the thesis that number-statements are statements about concepts. These two principles were to remain at the heart of Frege's thinking for many years to come, while he strove to perfect a symbolic and rigorous presentation of the logicist thesis.

It will be seen that Frege's philosophy of mathematics is closely linked to his understanding of several key terms of logic and of philosophy; and indeed in *Concept Script* and *Foundations* Frege not only founded modern logic, but also gave a fresh start to the philosophy of logic. He did so by making a sharp distinction between the philosophical treatment of logic and two other disciplines with which it had often been intermingled. He separated it, on the one hand, from psychology (with which it had often been confused by philosophers in the empiricist tradition) and, on the other hand, from epistemology (with which it is sometimes conflated by philosophers in the tradition stemming from Descartes).

For the nine years after the publication of *Foundations* Frege worked principally on his logicist project of deriving arithmetic from logic. His publications during this period, however, are especially concerned with problems in the philosophy of language. Three papers appeared in 1891-2: 'Function and Concept', 'Sense and Reference', 'Concept and Object'. Each of these authoritative essays presented philosophical ideas of fundamental importance with astonishing brevity and clarity. They were seen, no doubt, by Frege as ancillary to the logicist project, but at the present time they are regarded as founding classics of modern semantic theory.

One of the most significant developments in Frege's thoughts at this time was a new distinction which he now introduced between *sense* and *reference*. Where other philosophers talked ambiguously of the *meaning* of an expression, Frege invited us to mark a difference between the *reference* of an expression (the object to which it refers, as the planet Venus is the reference of 'The Morning Star') and the *sense* of an expression. ('The Evening Star' differs in sense from 'The Morning Star' though it too, as astronomers discovered, refers to Venus.) The most puzzling and controversial application of Frege's distinction between sense and reference was his theory that it was not only individual words that had reference, but also whole sentences. The reference of a sentence was its truth-value (that is, the True, or the False).

The climax of Frege's career as a philosopher should have been the publication of the volumes of *Grundgesetze der Arithmetik* (*The Basic Laws of Arithmetic*),[3] in which he set out to present in formal manner the logicist construction of arithmetic on the basis of pure logic. This work was intended to execute the task which had been sketched in the earlier books on the philosophy of mathematics: it was to enunciate a set of axioms which would be recognizably truths of logic, to propound a set of undoubtedly sound rules of inference, and then to present, one by one, derivations by these rules from these axioms of the standard truths of arithmetic, in an expanded version of the symbolism of *Concept Script*. However, no publisher would print the manuscript as a whole; Pohle of Jena, who had published 'Function and Concept' as a pamphlet, was willing to publish it in two volumes, the publication of the second instalment being conditional on the success of the first. Late in 1893

---

3. I shall refer to this work by its German title, since it has never been fully translated into English.

the first volume appeared; the publication of the second was delayed until 1903.

Grundgesetze follows in the main the lines of *The Foundations of Arithmetic*. However, much more emphasis is placed on the notion of class, which is now regarded as essential to the definition of the notion of number. The cardinal numbers are, in effect, defined as classes of equivalent classes, that is, classes with the same number of members; thus the number two is the class of pairs, and the number three is the class of trios. Despite appearances, this definition is not circular, because we can say what is meant by two classes having the same number of members without making use of the notion of number. Two classes are equivalent to each other if they can be mapped one-to-one onto each other. We can define the number zero in purely logical terms as the class of all classes equivalent to the class of objects which are not identical with themselves. We can define the number one as the class of all classes equivalent to the class whose only member is zero. In order to pass from definitions of zero and one to the definition of the other natural numbers, Frege makes use of the definitions of 'successor' and of other mathematical relations within the number series which he had developed in *Concept Script*. A treatment of negative, fractional, irrational and complex numbers was postponed until the second volume.

Frege's magnificent project aborted before it was completed. The first volume was received in general with the chill silence which had greeted his earlier works. As a result of this, publication of the second volume was held up for a decade and it had eventually to be published at the author's own expense. Publication of the first volume did, however, lead to Frege's promotion to a senior professorship at Jena and to a substantial research grant from the foundation set up by the Zeiss camera company. It also led to a fruitful controversy with the Italian logician Giuseppe Peano, who modified his own newly published axiomatization of arithmetic to take account of Frege's criticisms. Through Peano, Frege's work was brought to the notice of the first of his English readers, Bertrand Russell, who was at that time a young Fellow of Trinity College, Cambridge.

Frege occupied much of the time between the appearance of the two volumes of *Grundgesetze* in publishing increasingly bitter and sarcastic attacks on the scholars who had misunderstood his own publications. The most fruitful of these was his hostile review of the *Philosophie der Arithmetik* by the German philosopher Edmund Husserl; this was taken in good part by Husserl, who was converted by it from the psychologism which he had earlier defended, and he joined Frege as one of its severest critics.

While the second volume was in press, in 1902, Frege received a letter from Russell pointing out that the fifth of the initial axioms of *Grundgesetze* made the whole system inconsistent. This axiom states in effect that if every F is a G, and every G is an F, then the class of Fs is identical with the class of Gs, and vice versa: it was the axiom which, in Frege's words, allowed 'the transition from a concept to its extension', the transition which was essential if it was to be established that numbers were logical objects. Frege's system, with this axiom, permitted the formation of the class of all classes that are not members of themselves. But the formation of such a class, Russell pointed out, leads to paradox: if it is a member of itself then it is not a member of itself; if it is not a member of itself, then it is a member of itself. A system which leads to such a paradox cannot be logically sound.

With good reason, Frege was utterly downcast by this discovery, though he strove to patch his system by weakening the guilty axiom. The paradox and its attempted solution were described in an appendix to the second volume of *Grundgesetze* when it appeared in 1903. Frege's revised system, in its turn, proved inconsistent, though Frege continued to believe in it for some years yet. After his retirement from Jena in 1918 he seems at last to have given up his belief that arithmetic was derivable from logic, and to have returned to the view of Kant that arithmetic, like geometry, is synthetic a priori.

In the last years of his life, between 1918 and his death, Frege attempted to write a full treatise of philosophical logic. All that was completed was a series of articles (*Logical Investigations*, 1919–23) in which he returned to the relationship between logic and philosophical psychology, or the philosophy of mind, and discussed the nature of thought and inference.

Much of what Frege wrote on philosophical logic in his last years remained unpublished at his death. Frege and his wife Margaret had several children, all of whom died young; some time before her death in 1905 they adopted a son, Alfred, who became an engineer. When Frege made his will in January 1925 he left his unpublished papers to Alfred, with the following note:

> Dear Alfred,
> Do not despise the pieces I have written. Even if all is not gold, there is gold in them. I believe there are things here which will one day be prized much more highly than they are now. Take care that nothing gets lost.
> Your loving father
> It is a large part of myself which I bequeath to you herewith.[4]

Six months later Frege died, unaware that he would come to be regarded as the founder of the most influential philosophical movement of the twentieth century. His death was barely noticed by the learned world.

---

4. Most of Frege's posthumous papers were published in German in 1969 and in English in 1979.

CHAPTER 2

CONCEPT SCRIPT, I

In 1879 Frege published a pamphlet with the title *'Begriffschrift'*, which we can render into English as *Concept Script*. This pamphlet marked an epoch in the history of logic, for within its small compass – little more than a hundred pages – Frege set forth a new calculus which has a permanent place at the heart of modern logic. In presenting this calculus he also made a number of profound remarks about the nature of logic, proof and language which repay attentive study.

Frege presented his calculus in a symbolism invented for the purpose, the concept script which gave his book its title. The construction of this symbolism was originally motivated by Frege's desire to establish with certainty the true nature of arithmetic. The laws of logic operate in every sphere of knowledge. Now do proofs in arithmetic rest purely on these laws of logic, or do they need support from empirical facts? To answer this question, we have to see 'how far one could get in arithmetic by means of logical deductions alone, supported only by the laws of thought'.

In working on this task, Frege found ordinary language insufficiently precise for his purpose. Accordingly, he invented his concept script. In doing so, his aim was to strip language of all features which were irrelevant to the validity of proofs, since it was this which was the object of his study. The elements of sentences essential for inference constitute, in Frege's terminology, 'conceptual content'; it was for this reason that his new notation, designed to symbolize this and this alone, was called 'concept script'.

Arithmetic, geometry and chemistry already had, when Frege wrote, their own special symbolic notations. What was special about the concept script was that it was intended to be a single notation applicable in every field which makes use of rigorous proofs. In some fields – arithmetic perhaps – this new notation might be enough in itself to capture all that was necessary to test the validity of proof. In other fields – geometry or kinematics, say – a supplementary symbolism would be necessary to express the specific properties and relations involved. As physics progresses, new symbolic systems will no doubt be necessary to capture new discoveries; but the laws of logic operate in physics as elsewhere, and to codify these laws we do not have to wait until some mythical date when all the laws of nature will have been discovered.

Frege was not under the illusion that his concept script was a new and perfect language which would show up natural languages as imperfect. On the contrary, he thought that the relationship between his concept script and ordinary language was like the relationship between the microscope and the eye. The eye is greatly superior to the microscope: it can operate in many ways, and on many objects, where the microscope is useless. It is only where sharp resolution is needed for particular purposes that the microscope has the advantage over the unaided eye. Similarly, the concept script is devised for the special task of bringing into sharp focus those elements which are essential for the validity of proof. For this particular purpose, ordinary language is unwieldy, and the forms of expression of natural languages can be misleading. Frege hoped his concept script would help to unmask illusions generated by misleading idiom. In this sense it would help philosophy to 'break the power of the word over the human mind' (CN, p. 106).

When Frege says that ordinary language is deceptive, he does not mean that ordinary speakers are led into error in their everyday use of language, but that grammarians analyse language in ways which are misleading for logical purposes. One example is the distinction between the subject and the predicate of a sentence. Consider the two following sentences about the Battle of Hastings:

> William defeated Harold.
> Harold was defeated by William.

In school grammar we learn, or used to learn, that these two sentences are quite different from each other, having different subjects and different predicates. The subject of the first sentence is 'William' and the predicate (which might be further analysed into active verb and object) is 'defeated Harold'; the subject of the second sentence is 'Harold' and the predicate (which might be further analysed into passive verb and agent) is 'was defeated by William'.

There are indeed differences of linguistic importance between active and passive constructions. The choice between the two will depend, Frege says, on the context of 'interaction of speaker and listener': a speaker may choose one or other term as the subject for the sake of emphasis, or in order to link the sentence with what has gone before. But the differences between the two sentences have nothing to do with what follows from them logically. Anything which follows from the first follows from the second and vice versa. Hence, Frege says, two such sentences do not differ in conceptual content.

'A distinction between subject and predicate', Frege wrote in *Concept Script*, 'finds no place in my way of expressing a judgement' (CN, p. 112). In his later work, Frege went back to using the term 'predicate', employing it in a different sense from that which has been just illustrated. We may use the expressions 'grammatical subject' and 'grammatical predicate' to indicate the distinction which Frege dispensed with in his concept script, and use 'predicate' *tout court* in the sense in which he himself employed it in his later writings.

In the *Concept Script* Frege replaced the notions of *grammatical subject* and *grammatical predicate* with the logical concepts of *argument* and *function* (CN, p. 107). Suppose that we take our sentence

William defeated Harold

and put into it, in place of the word 'Harold', the word 'Canute'.
Clearly this alters the content of the sentence, and indeed it
turns it from a true sentence into a false sentence. We can think
of the sentence as in this way consisting of a constant component
'William defeated . . .'. and a replaceable symbol 'Harold'. The
name 'Harold' is replaceable by other similar symbols, by names
which name other people in the same way as 'Harold' names
Harold. If we think of a sentence in this way, Frege will call the
first, fixed, component a function, and the second component
the argument of the function.

The sentence 'William defeated Harold' is the result of completing the expression 'William defeated . . .' with the name 'Harold',
and the sentence 'William defeated Canute' is the result of
completing the same expression with the name 'Canute'. That is
to say, in the terminology suggested by *Concept Script*, the
sentence 'William defeated Harold' is the value of the function
'William defeated . . .' for the argument 'Harold', and 'William
defeated Canute' is the value of the same function for the
argument 'Canute'.

Like the distinction between subject and predicate, the distinction between function and argument does not affect the conceptual content. Just as two sentences with different subjects and
predicates may have the same conceptual content, so may two
sentences which are the values of different functions and different
arguments. Indeed, a single sentence, while retaining the same
conceptual content, may be analysed in more than one way into
function and argument. Thus the sentence

William defeated Harold

is not only the value of the function 'William defeated . . .' for
the argument 'Harold'; it is also the value of the function
'. . . defeated Harold' for the argument 'William'.

The expressions 'William defeated . . .' and '. . . defeated
Harold' each need just a single name to turn them into a

sentence; they are, in Frege's terminology, functions taking a single argument. But the expression '... defeated ...' needs to be supplemented at each end to turn it into a sentence: it is a function taking two arguments. 'William defeated Harold' is the value of this function for the arguments 'William' and 'Harold'. Clearly, it makes a great difference in which order the arguments occur, and any concept script will have to make provision for representing the order of their occurrence (CN, p. 128).

Consider now a rather special sentence which Frege draws to our attention:

Cato killed Cato.

We can consider this as a function of the argument 'Cato' in more than one way. It makes a difference whether we think of 'Cato' as replaceable by another argument at the first or the second or at both places. In the first case, '... killed Cato' is the function; in the second place 'Cato killed ...' is the function. In the third case '... killed ...' is the function, but we must find some way to indicate that the two gaps are to be filled with the same name, say by putting the same letter into each gap as a place-holder thus: 'X killed X'. This last expression will be tantamount to the expression '... killed himself' (or, in the case of an argument such as 'Cleopatra', tantamount to '... killed herself').

Frege offers the following general definition of 'function' and 'argument':

Suppose that a simple or complex symbol occurs in one or more places in an expression ... If we imagine this symbol as replaceable by another (the same one each time) at one or more of its occurrences, then the part of the expression that shows itself invariant under such replacement is called the function; and the replaceable part, the argument of the function. (CN, p. 127.)

This definition can be applied in the analysis not only of sentences, as in our previous examples, but also of expressions of other kinds, for instance complex names or descriptions.

'Father of Isaac', for instance, a description of Abraham, can be regarded as the value of the function 'Father of . . .' for the argument 'Isaac'.

In *Concept Script* it is tolerably clear that functions and arguments and their values are all bits of language: names, simple or complex, and sentences, with or without gaps. The definition offered by Frege explicitly refers to expressions, not to the things outside language which give content or meaning to expressions. His examples of arguments and functions are in general introduced in quotation marks, which would naturally indicate that it is linguistic items which are being talked about.

However, in using the terms 'function' and 'argument' Frege was borrowing a mathematical usage; and an analysis of the usage of mathematicians shows that for them functions and arguments are not linguistic items, but something different. In the equation

$$y = x(x - 4)$$

a mathematician may say that y indicates the value of a certain function, and x indicates the argument of the function. The value of the function in question, for the argument 8, is 32. But here argument and value are not symbols: they are numbers, not numerals. In his later work Frege became much more interested in applying the notions of *function* and *argument* not so much to items of language, but to the items which language is used to express and talk about. Later, we will follow that more extensive interest of Frege's. Here in *Concept Script* the interest is only latent: the principal concern is in applying the notions to the construction of sentences in natural language and in symbolic notation.[1]

---

1. In *Concept Script* Frege was not as careful as he later became to distinguish systematically between signs and what they signified – between, for instance, the name 'William' and the person William the Conqueror whom the name names. In talking of functions he occasionally lapses from his stated view that they are bits of language and implies that they are something lying behind language, for example, concepts. Thus, in giving the third possible analysis of 'Cato killed Cato', he says, 'if we imagine "Cato" as replaceable at both occurrences, then

To avoid confusion with the functions and arguments which later occupied Frege's main interest we may call the functions of *Concept Script* 'linguistic functions' and 'linguistic arguments'.[2] In the present chapter, whenever I use the word 'function', I should be taken to mean 'linguistic function'. In later chapters, if I wish to talk about linguistic functions I will identify them explicitly as such.

In simple sentences the distinction between a function and its argument is irrelevant to the conceptual content just as the distinction between subject and predicate was. In what way, then, is the function/argument dichotomy logically more appropriate than the subject/predicate distinction? The answer is that it provides a more flexible method of bringing out logically relevant similarities between sentences. Subject–predicate analysis is sufficient to mark the similarity between 'Caesar conquered Gaul' and 'Caesar defeated Pompey', but it is blind to the similarity between 'Caesar conquered Gaul' and 'Pompey avoided Gaul'. This becomes a matter of logical importance when we deal with sentences in which there occur, instead of proper names like 'Caesar' and 'Gaul', expressions containing words like 'all' or 'some': expressions such as 'all Romans' or 'some province'. Once we introduce such expressions, the distinction between function and argument does, in fact, become relevant to conceptual content. This is something which we will explore later (see p. 25).

In the centuries preceding Frege the most important part of logic was the study of the validity of inferences containing sentences beginning with 'all', 'no' and 'some'. Consider the following two inferences:

"killing oneself" is the function'. This seems confused. The use of quotation marks in 'killing oneself' makes it look as if Frege is, consistently, talking of a linguistic expression; but 'killing oneself' is not the same linguistic expression as 'X killed X', even if one might want to say that both are expressions of the same concept.

2. Here I follow Geach in G. E. M. Anscombe and P. T. Geach, *Three Philosophers*, p. 143.

(1)   All Greeks are Europeans.
            Some Greeks are male.
            Therefore, some Europeans are male.

and

(2)   All cows are mammals.
            Some mammals are quadrupeds.
            Therefore, all cows are quadrupeds.

These two inferences have a lot in common with each other. They are both inferences which draw a conclusion from a pair of premisses. In each inference a keyword which appears in the grammatical-subject place of the conclusion appears in one of the premisses, and a keyword which appears in the grammatical predicate of the conclusion appears in the other premiss. Inferences displaying this feature are called, by logicians, 'syllogisms'; and the branch of logic which studies the validity of inferences of this kind, which was initiated by Aristotle, is called 'syllogistic'.

A valid inference is an inference of a form which will never lead from true premisses to a false conclusion. Of the two inferences set out above, the first is valid and the second is invalid. It is true that in each of the cases given the premisses are true and the conclusion is true. One cannot fault the second inference on the ground that the sentences occurring in it are false. What one can fault is the 'Therefore': the conclusion may be true, but it does not follow from the premisses.

We can bring this out by constructing a parallel inference which leads from true premisses to a false conclusion. For instance,

(3)   All whales are mammals.
            Some mammals are land-animals.
            Therefore, all whales are land-animals.

This inference is of the same form as inference (2), as can be brought out by exhibiting the structure of the inference by schematic letters:

(4)   All *A*s are *B*s.
                Some *B*s are *C*s.
                Therefore all *A*s are *C*s.

Because inference (3) leads from true premises to a false conclusion, we can see that the argument-form of (4) cannot be relied upon. Hence, inference (2), though its conclusion is in fact true, is not a valid inference.

One way to define logic is to say that it is the discipline which sorts out good inferences from bad. Logic before Frege offered a fairly complicated set of rules which would sort out good syllogisms from bad syllogisms. There is no point here in giving examples of those rules; it is enough to say that they were sufficient to settle that inference (1) is a valid inference, and that inference (2) is an invalid one.

The weakness of syllogistic was that it could not cope with inferences in which words like 'all' or 'some' (or 'every' and 'any') occurred not in the subject place but somewhere in the grammatical predicate. The rules would not permit one to determine, for instance, the validity of inferences containing premisses such as 'every schoolchild knows some dates' or 'some people hate all policemen' in cases where the inference turned on the word 'some' in the first sentence, or the word 'all' in the second. Frege's *Concept Script* showed how to overcome this difficulty.

The first step was to introduce a new notation to express the kind of generality expressed by a word such as 'all', no matter where it occurred in the sentence. Suppose we take the sentence 'Socrates is mortal'. We can analyse this into an argument and a function, 'Socrates' being the argument, and '. . . is mortal' being the function. If 'Socrates is mortal' is a true sentence, we might say that the function holds true[3] for the argument 'Socrates'.

---

3. It is thus that I translate the German expression corresponding to 'is a fact' in the Geach and Bynum translations.

Frege introduced a symbol to signify that a certain function held true no matter what we took its argument to be. The actual symbolism he introduced is no longer used by logicians; using a modern equivalent instead we can write

$$(x) \ (x \text{ is mortal}).$$

The '(x)' is the sign for generality, and the whole expression can be read 'For all x, x is mortal', where this is to be taken to mean that no matter what name is attached as an argument to the function '. . . is mortal', the function holds true. Let us, for the time being, and for the sake of exposition, restrict our attention to names which are names of human beings. With that restriction, the sentence 'For all x, x is mortal' will be equivalent, in conceptual content, to the sentence which in ordinary language is the generalization of 'Socrates is mortal', namely 'Everyone is mortal'.

Similarly, if we take a sentence such as 'John is related to Jane' we can generalize it in accordance with the various possible ways in which we have seen it can be analysed into function and argument. Thus, '$(x) \ (x$ is related to Jane)' is equivalent to 'Everyone is related to Jane' and '$(y) \ (John$ is related to $y)$' is equivalent to 'John is related to everyone'. If we analyse the sentence by means of the two-place function '. . . is related to . . .' we will need two marks of generality if we wish to generalize in the case of both arguments. Thus we should write '$(x) \ (y) \ (x$ is related to $y)$', which is to be read 'For all x and for all y, x is related to y', and it is equivalent to 'everyone is related to everyone'. It was principally because his notation thus enabled him to give uniform expression to generality wherever and however often it occurred in a sentence that Frege was able to make great advances on the traditional syllogistic.

Frege did not introduce a special sign to correspond to the word 'some' in a sentence such as 'some Romans were cowards'. It had long been accepted by logicians that this sentence was equivalent to 'not all Romans were not cowards'; and Frege made use of this relationship between 'some' and 'not all . . . not' in order to codify sentences containing 'some'. To do this it is necessary to have a symbol corresponding to 'not'.

Frege introduced a negation sign, a sign which if attached to a sentence 'expresses the circumstance of the [sentence's] content not being the case' (CN, p. 120). Once again, the particular symbol he introduced has passed out of use, but we may use one of its modern equivalents, the sign '¬'. Using this symbol, we write the negation of 'Socrates is mortal' as '¬ (Socrates is mortal)', which can be read as 'It is not the case that Socrates is mortal'. (This is equivalent to 'Socrates is not mortal'; but it goes along with Frege's rejection of the grammatical subject–predicate distinction that he attaches the negation-sign, not to the grammatical predicate of a sentence, but to the sentence as a whole. We shall see the advantages of this method of symbolism later.)

Like the original sentence 'Socrates is mortal' the sentence which is the negation of it can be analysed into argument and function, for example, '¬ (Socrates is mortal)' is the value of the function '¬ (. . . is mortal)' for the argument 'Socrates'. As before, we can attach the sign of generality to this function and obtain the sentence '(x) ¬ $(x$ is mortal)', which can be read 'For all x, it is not the case that x is mortal', and this is equivalent in conceptual content to the ordinary language sentence 'Everyone is not mortal' interpreted in the sense of 'No one is mortal'.

However, the ordinary-language sentence can be taken in more than one way. 'Everyone is not mortal' might be read as being constructed in the same way as 'Everything that glisters is not gold', in which case it would mean the same as 'Not everyone is mortal'. This would have a different translation into Frege's concept script, as '¬ (x) $(x$ is mortal)', which means that it is not the case that for all x, x is mortal. Here we have an example of the way in which Frege believed that his script was more precise than ordinary language, and he enabled us to disambiguate sentences which in ordinary language might be read in more than one way (CN, p. 133–4).

The difference, which is obscure in ordinary language and is clarified by the concept script, is called by Frege a difference of *scope*. In '⌐ (x) (x is mortal)' the sign of negation is outside the scope of the sign of generalization: the negation is not generalized. In '(x) ⌐ (x is mortal)' the negation-sign comes within the scope of the sign of generalization, and the negation is generalized (CN, p. 131). We have here a distinction between the negation of a generalization, and the generalization of a negation.

The expression 'some' can now be defined in terms of negation and generalization. 'Someone is mortal' can be taken as equivalent to 'It is not the case that everyone is not mortal', or, in our modernization of Frege's concept script, '⌐ (x) ⌐ (x is mortal)'.

Hitherto, for purposes of exposition, I have limited the replacement of 'x's in Frege's concept script to the names of human beings. Frege himself made no such restriction; he thought that objects of all kinds were nameable – numerals, for instance, were the names of numbers – and the argument places in his concept script can be filled with the name of anything whatever. Consequently '(x) (x is mortal)' is really to be read not as 'Everyone is mortal' but as 'Everything is mortal' – a proposition which is untrue because, for instance, the number ten is not mortal.

Frege's concept script allows us to make statements about the existence of things of particular kinds. We use the same notation as that used above for making statements containing the expression 'some'. Frege observes that '⌐ (x) ⌐ (x is a house)' is equivalent to 'there are houses', provided that this sentence is understood as covering the case where there is only one house and no more (CN, p. 134). It is possible, though Frege does not do so, to introduce a single symbol to abbreviate '⌐ (x) ⌐', and this symbol would thus be equivalent to 'some'. The symbols thus equivalent to 'all' and 'some' are now called 'quantifiers' by logicians, and the branch of logic which concerns their use in inferences is known as quantification theory.

It was Frege who first fully systematized quantification theory. We have seen that logicians before Frege used schematic letters to bring out the structure of propositions entering into syllogisms. Frege adopted and extended this use. To indicate a function of the argument X without specifying it, Frege in *Concept Script* writes a Greek letter followed by an 'X' in parentheses. We can say in general that to assert that $\Phi(X)$ is, roughly, to assert that X has the property Φ. To indicate, without specifying, a function of two arguments X and Y, we write $\Psi(X, Y)$, where the places of X and Y within the parentheses represent the places occupied by X and Y in the function. Thus to assert that $\Psi(X, Y)$ is, roughly, to assert that X has the relation Ψ to Y.[4]

At this point Frege makes a brief remark: it is of great importance but its importance is not apparent on first reading. He says that since the symbol 'Φ' occurs at a particular place in the expression '$\Phi(X)$', and since we can imagine it being replaced by other symbols, such as 'Ψ', in order to express different functions of the argument X, *we may regard $\Phi(X)$ as a function of the argument* Φ. Note that he is not saying that we may, if we wish, regard 'X' as the function and 'Φ' as the argument in '$\Phi(X)$' (that would make nonsense of the distinction he has made so carefully). What he is doing is moving to a different level of analysis. He is saying that just as, at the basic level, 'Φ' is a function of the argument 'X', so, if we move up from considering the relation between one part and another part of a sentence to considering the relation between the parts and the whole sentence, we can say that the whole sentence is a

---

4. In Frege's exposition at this point (CN, p. 129) there is some confusion since 'Φ' is meant to be a variable replaceable by a linguistic function, such as '... is mortal'. To speak, therefore, of 'having the property Φ' involves a confusion between a sign and what it signifies. If we assert that Socrates is mortal we do not assert that he has the property '... is mortal' but that he has the property of mortality. In his later work Frege was to address the problems inherent in this analysis. A separate point is that Frege says that '$\Psi(A,B)$' is translatable as 'B stands in the Ψ-relation to A', reversing the order of the argument places. He subsequently abandoned this confusing practice.

function of the function contained in it. A function of this kind, a function of a function, we might appropriately call a second-level function.

At first sight, this is puzzling. When Frege introduced the notion, he defined a function as a part of an expression. But '$\Phi(X)$' corresponds not to a partial but to a complete expression, a whole sentence. The answer to the puzzle must be that Frege thinks that there is a way in which '$\Phi(X)$' can be supplemented to make a greater whole, in the way in which 'Φ' is supplemented by 'X' to make the whole sentence '$\Phi(X)$'. To see what this means, we have to look at what Frege says to link together his terminology of argument and function with his method of symbolizing generality.

Frege wrote:

Let me warn here against an illusion to which the use of ordinary language easily gives rise. If we compare two propositions:

'The number 20 can be represented as the sum of four squares.'

and

'Every positive integer can be represented as the sum of four squares.' it appears possible to consider 'being representable as the sum of four squares' as a function whose argument is 'the number 20' one time, and 'every positive integer' the other time. We may see that this view is mistaken if we observe that 'the number 20' and 'every positive integer' are not concepts of the same rank. (CN, p. 128.)

As one way of explaining what he meant by saying that the two expressions differed in rank, Frege said that whereas 'the number 20' yielded an independent idea, the expression 'every positive integer' acquires a sense only in the context of a sentence. If function and argument are completely determinate, the way in which the sentence is analysed into argument and function is irrelevant to the conceptual content. But this is not so if the argument is indeterminate. 'Every positive integer can be represented as the sum of four squares', translated in terms of function and argument, is equivalent to 'whatever name of a

25

positive integer you take as argument for the function "... is representable as the sum of four squares", the resulting sentence is always true'.[5] In such a case, Frege says, the distinction between argument and function begins to be relevant to content.

The justification for this remark becomes clear if we look at the representation of such a sentence in Frege's own concept script. For simplicity's sake, let us assume that we are talking simply about the universe of positive integers. With respect to that universe, the Fregean formula '$(x) \Phi (x)$', if we treat 'Φ' as an abbreviation for 'can be represented as the sum of four squares', corresponds to the sentence 'Every positive integer can be represented as the sum of four squares.' But this formula can be broken up into argument and function in only one way. The first '(x)' is not an argument but a sign of generality. The 'x' in the second pair of parentheses is not an argument but a variable, that is to say, a symbol showing the point at which an argument can be introduced. The only symbol which can be regarded as an argument is the function symbol 'Φ'. The whole sentence, then, can be regarded as the value of the function '$(x) (\ldots x)$' for the argument 'Φ'. The function $(x) (\ldots x)$, being a function of a function, that is to say a function taking a function as its argument, will be a second-level function.

In Frege's concept script, as in our modernization of it, the difference in rank between an expression such as 'the number 20' and 'every positive integer' is brought out by a difference in the style of symbol used to correspond to the expressions in natural language. What Frege calls a determinate argument will, in our version of his script, be represented by an upper-case italic letter (e.g. 'X'); what he calls an indeterminate argument

5. Here I paraphrase Frege to make what he says consistent with the theory of linguistic functions presented in *Concept Script*. His own formulation 'Whatever arbitrary positive integer you may take as argument for "being representable as the sum of four squares", the proposition always remains true' (CN, p. 128) involves, in the context of the stated theory of *Concept Script*, a confusion between signs and things signified.

will be represented by a lower-case italic letter variable (for example, the 'x' that occurs in the quantifier and in the sign showing the argument place of the function which occurs within the scope of the quantifier).[6]

We can now see how to answer the question: Why did Frege think that '$\Phi(X)$' could be regarded as a function of 'Φ' even though '$\Phi(X)$' is complete and a function is something incomplete? A first-level function, such as '. . . is mortal', is incomplete. But there are two different ways in which it can be completed. It can be completed by having an argument inserted in its argument place, as in 'Socrates is mortal'. Or it can be completed by itself becoming the argument of a second-level function. This is what happens when the ellipsis in '. . . is mortal' is filled with a quantifier such as 'Everything'.

To complete our sketch of Frege's theory of quantification, we have to move from considering the quantifiers themselves to considering other expressions of natural language, and their equivalents in concept script, whose job is to link one proposition to another rather than to construct individual propositions. The most important of these is the sign of conditionality, which corresponds to 'if' in ordinary language.

Suppose that there are two propositions 'p' and 'q'. If we are called upon to make a judgement about them, there are four possible lines we might wish to take. We might wish:

(1)	To affirm p and to affirm q,
(2)	To affirm p and to deny q,
(3)	To deny p and to affirm q,
(4)	To deny p and to deny q.

Frege introduces a sign, which we may render as '→', whose

6. In Frege's own script there are two kinds of lower-case letter variables: Gothic letters, whose scope is determined by a quantifier containing the same letter, and italic letters, whose scope extends over the entire proposition in which they occur.

purpose he explains roughly as follows. Someone who asserts '$q \rightarrow p$' wishes to renounce option (3) and retain the other three options.

Modern logicians operate with a sign whose function in the calculus is very much the same as Frege's sign. But they explain its operation in terms of truth and falsity rather than in terms of affirmation and denial. This makes it much clearer to explain.[7] The four possibilities for 'p' and 'q' are now:

(1) p is true and q is true,
(2) p is true and q is false,
(3) p is false and q is true,
(4) p is false and q is false,

and '$q \rightarrow p$' is true, on this account, just in case the third possibility does not hold (in which case one of the other three cases hold).

Some logicians have offered '$q \rightarrow p$' as equivalent to 'if q then p'. If we accept this equivalence, then the following propositions come out true:

If the sun is shining, $3 \times 7 = 21$.
If perpetual motion is possible, the world is infinite.
If the Moon is in quadrature with the Sun then the Moon
    appears semicircular.

These propositions are suggested by examples given by Frege to illustrate the import of this symbol for conditionality; but Frege himself here denies that in the first two cases the word 'if' of natural language is appropriate.[8] The first case is one where

---

7. Frege's procedure here seems to involve a confusion of logic and psychology of a kind which he would later reject with contempt. Later in the *Concept Script*, there are some better inspired passages where he asks not whether p is affirmed and q is denied, but whether *p is to be* affirmed and *q is to be* denied. In my exposition in the text, taking my cue from these passages, I have tried to paraphrase his teaching in a way which avoids the confusion while being as faithful as possible to his intention.

8. He was later to modify his position on this issue; see p. 205.

we would affirm '$q \rightarrow p$' simply because we would unconditionally affirm 'p'; the second is a case where we would affirm '$q \rightarrow p$' simply because we would unconditionally deny 'q'. The third case, he says, represents a judgement which one might make without knowing whether 'p' or 'q' were to be affirmed or denied. It is in this case alone, he suggests, that it is appropriate to render '$q \rightarrow p$' as 'if q then p'. The causal connection implicit in the word 'if' is, he says, 'not expressed by our symbolism'. There are connections other than causal ones that may be expressed by 'if' (I may use the word, for instance, to express a logical connection, a geometrical connection, or a conditional resolve I have made). Frege's sign does not express these connections either: it does not represent any connection between the content of the sentences which it links, but only between their truth and falsehood.

Frege's sign is related to the word 'if' in the way in which, in general, expressions in Frege's concept script are related to expressions in natural language. That is to say, it can be looked on as a stripped-down version of the word 'if', designed to capture just that aspect of its meaning which is necessary for the formulation of rigorous proofs containing it. If we know that 'if q then p' is true then we know at least that it is not the case that q is true and p is false. This minimum of content, Frege claimed, is all that we need in order to express rigorously the chains of reasoning necessary in logic and arithmetic.

We may analyse a proposition which is formed by linking two propositions with the '$\rightarrow$' sign into function and argument, just as we earlier analysed simple propositions. Frege does not explicitly do this in *Concept Script*, though he was to do so in later writing. The function '$\ldots \rightarrow \ldots$' takes sentences as its arguments, just as '$\ldots$ is mortal' was a function which took names as its arguments. 'It is night $\rightarrow$ it is dark' is the value of the function '$\ldots \rightarrow \ldots$' (which we might equally well write '$p \rightarrow q$') for the arguments 'it is night' and 'it is dark'. The function '$p \rightarrow q$' is a function whose values and arguments are both sentences. It is a function which has a particular property: whether the sentence which is its value is true or false will depend on nothing other than whether the sentences which are its arguments are true or false. Functions of this kind were later named, by Bertrand Russell, 'truth-functions'.

The conditional is not the only truth-function. Negation, represented by the sign '$\neg$', is a truth-function, since a negated sentence is true just in case the sentence negated is false, and vice versa. Whereas the conditional is a truth-function of two arguments, negation is a truth-function of a single argument. But there are other truth-functions of two arguments. A conjunction ('p and q') is the value of a function whose arguments are the two conjoined sentences; it is true if both its arguments are true, and otherwise it is false. A disjunction ('p or q') may be regarded as true if at least one of its arguments are true, and false if they are both false.[9]

Frege (unlike some later logicians) did not introduce special symbols for conjunction and disjunction, related to 'and' and 'or' in the way in which '$\rightarrow$' is related to 'if', though he recognized the possibility of doing this (CN, p. 123). Instead, he expressed conjunction and disjunction by using his signs for negation and conditionality. Thus, '$\neg q \rightarrow p$' is used when we wish to rule out the case in which p is to be denied and the negation of q is to be affirmed; it is, Frege says, equivalent to 'p and q cannot both be denied'; and this is the meaning which he attaches to 'p or q'. Likewise, '$q \rightarrow \neg p$' is to be used if we wish to rule out the case in which the negation of p is to be denied and q is to be affirmed. If we negate this in turn, we get '$\neg(q \rightarrow \neg p)$' which can be translated as 'p and q'.

Frege would use the same expression '$\neg(q \rightarrow \neg p)$' to translate '$p$ but q' as well as 'p and q'. He observes, however, that in ordinary language 'p but q' differs from 'p and q' in that it does not just express the joint truth of the two propositions; it also

9. Towards the end of his life, in his essay 'Compound Thoughts', Frege spelt these matters out in a much clearer and simpler manner, see p. 205.

hints that there is something unexpected about the fact that *q*. The difference between 'but' and 'and', however, is a feature of ordinary language which he does not attempt to reproduce in his symbolism.[10] A sentence compounded with 'but' will, he maintains, have the same conceptual content as one compounded with 'and'; and this conceptual content can be rendered, as explained above, by means of his signs for conditionality and negation (CN, p. 123).

It would be possible, as Frege says, to work the other way round. We could introduce a symbol for the truth-function of conjunction, say '&': '*p* & *q*' is to be true when *p* is true and when *q* is true, and otherwise false. Instead of introducing a sign for conditionality as a primitive symbol, we could define one in terms of '&': thus '*q* → *p*' could be defined as '¬(*q* & ¬*p*)'. This might, indeed, seem a more natural procedure. Frege says that he prefers to take the conditionality sign as basic because in the operation of logic deduction is more important than conjunction, and 'if ... then' and its symbolic surrogate seem to have a special relationship to deduction. This will become clearer in the next chapter, when we sketch Frege's own systematic development of logic.

Before we turn to that, however, there is one further important basic concept introduced by Frege in *Concept Script*. This is the notion of *identity of content*. He introduces a symbol '≡' which is defined thus: if we assert '*X* ≡ *Y*' we assert that the symbol '*X*' and the symbol '*Y*' have the same conceptual content, so that we can always replace '*X*' by '*Y*' and vice versa.

Several things must be noted about this definition. First, '≡' may stand between symbols of various kinds: in place of '*X*' and of '*Y*' we may write either complete sentences, or names, whether simple or complex. In discussing identity of content Frege uses 'name' to cover all these different kinds of symbol. Secondly, Frege draws attention to a special feature of the sign '≡'. The

---

10. He was later to call this feature 'colour'; see p. 183.

definition given above implies that the assertion of '$X \equiv Y$' is an assertion about names, not about their content. He writes:

Elsewhere, names are mere proxies for their content, and thus any phrase they occur in just expresses a relation between their various contents; but names at once appear *in propria persona* so soon as they are joined together by their symbol for identity of content; for this signifies the circumstance that the two names have the same content. (CN, p. 124.)

It might be thought that in a perfect language there would only be a single symbol answering to each distinguishable content. In that case, there would be no need for a symbol for identity of content, and such a symbol would be futile since the only true sentences containing it would be truisms of the form '$X \equiv X$'. But this is not so: a symbol for identity of content is needed because the same content may be determined in different ways; and it may be a significant judgement that two different modes of determination do give the same content.

Frege illustrates this with a geometrical example.[11] Suppose that *a*, *b*, *c* are the lines connecting the vertices of a triangle with the midpoints of the opposite sides. 'The point of intersection of *a* and *b*' and 'the point of intersection of *b* and *c*' are two different complex names. Yet both these names are names of the same point. In the terminology of *Concept Script*, they are names with the same content. The existence of different names with the same content is not an imperfection of language: mathematics would be enormously impoverished if one could not determine the same content in more than one way. In the simple example given, of course, the truth of the assertion 'The point of intersection of *a* and *b* $\equiv$ The point of intersection of *b* and *c*' is easily seen. More complicated equivalences may take long periods of work to establish.

11. The actual example used by Frege in CN is unnecessarily complex; I have used a simpler one drawn from CP, p. 158.

Frege's sign '≡' can be looked on as an extension of the arithmetical sign '='. The '=' of arithmetic can be placed between numerical expressions and can be used to indicate that the flanking expressions denote the same number. Frege's '≡' can be placed between expressions of the most varied kinds, and can be used to indicate that the flanking expressions name the same content, of whatever kind.

Frege says that if '$X ≡ Y$' can be truly asserted, then 'X' can always be replaced by 'Y', and conversely. What is the force of the 'can' here? Does Frege mean that if you take a sentence containing 'X' and replace 'X' with 'Y' you will have another sentence with the same content? Surely not. If Frege had asserted in *Concept Script*

The Queen of England ≡ The Empress of India

he would have made a true assertion (Queen Victoria had been given the title very shortly before he wrote). But the sentence surely does not have the same content as the following sentence, constructed from it by replacing 'The Empress of India' with the words 'The 'Queen of England'

The Queen of England ≡ The Queen of England.

This last sentence is an empty truism, whereas to make a judgement on the former one must know something of English constitutional history.

When Frege says that if 'X' and 'Y' have an identical content, then 'X' can be replaced with 'Y' in a sentence, what he must mean is not that the replacement will not affect the content of a sentence at all, but that it will not affect whether the sentence is true or false. He must mean that if we take a true sentence containing the words 'The Queen of England' and replace these words with 'The Empress of India', the sentence would remain true, and that similarly, a false statement will remain false after a similar replacement. As he would later express the matter, the sentence will retain its *truth-value* (that is, its truth or falsity, as the case may be) after the substitution. Frege was later to develop a special terminology – the pair of terms 'sense' and 'reference' – to make clear what is left ambiguous when he is operating only with the single term 'content' to express what a sentence signifies.

In the next chapter we will explain the system of logic which Frege constructed when he put to work the symbols he had invented for his concept script. My purpose in this chapter has been to present the apparatus of Frege's logic in such a way as to emphasize those elements of it which were to survive into his later writings and which remain operative in logic at the present time. This has meant playing down certain features of *Concept Script* which we can now clearly see to be muddled. That we can do so is partly due to Frege's own later work in which – as we shall see – a number of the confusions of *Concept Script* are identified and clarified.

One unsatisfactory feature of the system of *Concept Script*, however, is too important to be passed over and glossed by benevolent paraphrase. The very first new symbol which Frege introduces (CN, p. 111) is what he calls 'the judgement stroke'. He writes:

A judgement is always to be expressed by means of the sign

$$\vdash$$

This stands to the left of the symbol or complex of symbols giving the content of the judgement. If we omit the small vertical stroke at the left end of the horizontal stroke, then the judgement is to be transformed into a mere complex of ideas; the author is not expressing his acceptance or non-acceptance of its truth. For example, let

$$\vdash A$$

mean the judgement: 'unlike magnetic poles attract one another'. Then

$$— A$$

will not express this judgement; it is simply to evoke in the reader the idea of the mutual attraction of opposite magnetic poles – perhaps so that he may make inferences from the thought and use them to test its correctness. We paraphrase in this case by means of the words 'the circumstance that' or 'the proposition that'. (CN, p. 112.)

In his later work, Frege constantly emphasized the need to distinguish between logic and psychology. In this early passage, the distinction seems blurred. Frege is introducing a logical symbol, and yet he does so in psychological terms: for he defines the symbol in terms of a contrast between judgement and combinations of ideas. Now judgement is surely a mental act, and ideas are surely something in the mind.

Judging that *p*, we might say, is an act which is the mental equivalent of the speech-act of asserting that *p*; it is, to use the Biblical expression, 'saying in one's heart' that *p*. Frege says indifferently that the vertical stroke expresses a judgement and that it expresses an assertion. His symbol is now commonly referred to as his 'assertion sign'.[12]

It is true, and important, that there is a great difference between judging that *p*, and merely entertaining the thought that *p*. There is a similar difference between asserting that *p*, and merely propounding the proposition that *p*. A proposition may be propounded, as Frege says, as a hypothesis; or it may occur, unasserted, as part of another proposition. A contemporary philosopher has offered to bring out the utility of Frege's assertion sign in the following way.

Does '*p*' mean the same both times in '*m*, if *m* then *p*, *ergo p*', or again in 'not *m*, *m* or *p*, *ergo p*'? If it does, there is no inference, for the assertion '*p*' is already part of the premises; if it does not, the inference

12. In fact, as the paragraph quoted above shows, it was only the vertical part of that symbol which was to express judgement, or assertion; the horizontal line is what he calls 'the content stroke'. Its function, in his symbolism, is to bind together, in the appropriate way, the symbols which follow it. In the modernized version of Frege's symbolism used in this book, and in most modern expositions of Frege, it is superfluous. See Appendix I.

is vitiated by the ambiguity of 'p'. Frege would write such inferences as follows: '$\vdash m$, $\vdash$ (if m then p), ergo $\vdash p$'; '$\vdash$ (not m), $\vdash$ (m or p), *ergo* $\vdash p$'. The content asserted in '$\vdash p$' occurs also in the premiss '$\vdash$ (if m then p)' or '$\vdash$ (m or p)' but is not asserted in this latter context.[13]

This captures well, I believe, what Frege had in mind when he introduced the assertion sign. None the less, its introduction – as one can see with the benefit of Frege's later work – does involve a confusion between logic and what may broadly be called psychology. Whether I assert something, or judge something, is a matter of my mental history. It is the content of what is asserted that concerns logic – the conceptual content in Frege's own sense of that which is relevant to the drawing of inferences. If 'q' follows logically from 'p' then it does so whether or not I, or anyone else, actually assert that q, or actually judge that p.

As Frege says, the thought that unlike magnetic poles attract each other can be entertained without being judged. One might call this – though Frege would later see reason for not doing so – the complex idea of the mutual attraction of unlike poles. But if one does speak of this idea (which, being an idea, is something mental) one must distinguish it from the circumstance that unlike magnetic poles attract each other (which, if it obtains, obtains in the real world, not in the mind) and from the proposition that unlike poles attract each other (which, if we are to be guided by the German word 'Satz' in Frege's original, is something which is an item of language). The paragraph by Frege quoted above seems to lump together linguistic, mental and real-world items in a way which Frege would later come to regard with profound suspicion.

One merit which Frege would continue to see in his assertion sign was that it brought out the distinction between assertion and predication; it made manifest that attaching a predicate to a

---

13. Geach, in G. E. M. Anscombe and P. T. Geach, *Three Philosophers*, Blackwell, 1961, p. 133.

subject did not, as some earlier logicians had erroneously maintained, necessarily involve making an assertion about what the
subject named. In 'If the Labour Party wins the election, the
pound will be devalued', 'wins the election' is attached as grammatical predicate to 'the Labour Party' as grammatical subject,
but no assertion is made that the Labour party will win the
election.[14]

The most important point made by Frege in the context of the
introduction of the assertion sign is that negation, and the
distinction between universal and particular, belonged not with
the judgement or assertion, but rather to the possible content of
judgement. It was only in his later work that he expounded his
reasons for saying this; but his own development of logic in
Concept Script would be impossible if negation and quantification could not be applied to unasserted propositions.

14. In *Concept Script* Frege announced his intention to abandon the distinction
between subject and predicate; but he made an unfortunate modification of this
in connection with the assertion sign. He wrote as if the introduction of the
assertion sign amounted to the reduction of all predicates to the single predicate
'is a fact' (CN, p. 113). Thus 'Archimedes perished at the capture of Syracuse',
he said, could be expressed as 'the violent death of Archimedes at the capture of
Syracuse is a fact'. But this surely involves the incoherent notion that predication
includes assertion, the very confusion which Frege later saw it as the function of
the assertion sign to dispel.

CHAPTER 3

CONCEPT SCRIPT, II

In the previous chapter, we saw that Frege would symbolize a universal statement, such as 'Everything is mortal', by using his universal quantifier symbol:

$$(x) \, (x \text{ is mortal})$$

It is rare, in fact, for us to want to make statements of such unrestricted generality. It is much more common for us to want to say that everything *of a certain kind* has a certain property, or that everything which has a certain given property also has a certain other property. 'All men are mortal' or 'What goes up must come down' are examples of typical universal sentences of ordinary language.

Frege symbolizes such sentences by making use both of the sign of generality and the sign of conditionality. The expression

$$(x) \, (Fx \rightarrow Gx)$$

can be read

For all x, if Fx then Gx

Frege explains this in *Concept Script* as meaning that whatever may be put in place of 'x', there is never a case in which 'Fx' is to be affirmed and 'Gx' to be denied. Following the style of exposition he favoured later, we can gloss this expression more simply as: No matter what x may be, if 'Fx' is true then 'Gx' is true.

If we substitute 'is a man' for 'F', and 'is mortal' for 'G' then we obtain 'For all x, if x is a man, x is mortal', which is what Frege offers as the translation of 'All men are mortal' (CN,

p. 134). Similarly, if we substitute 'goes up' for '*F*' and 'must come down' for *G*, then we can obtain a translation into concept script of 'What goes up must come down'.

It is to be noted that the 'if' here is the truth-functional 'if'; 'if *Fx* then *Gx*' means no more than 'not both *Fx* and not *Gx*'. Hence, if there were no men, then 'For all *x*, if *x* is a man, *x* is mortal' would none the less be true; because '*Fx*' would be false no matter what we substituted for '*x*', and therefore there would be no possibility of producing a case where '*Fx*' was true and '*Gx*' was false. This point marks a difference between Frege's formulation and the natural language sentence 'All men are mortal'. Philosophers before Frege disagreed how to respond to the question whether 'All men are mortal' is true if there are no men; some argued for a positive and some for a negative answer. Frege's formulation adopts unambiguously one of the two possible interpretations of the ambiguous sentence of ordinary language.

The contradictory of 'All men are mortal' is 'Some men are not mortal'. This is symbolized by attaching the negation-sign to the formula for 'All men are mortal', thus

$$\neg(x)\ (x \text{ is a man} \rightarrow x \text{ is mortal}).$$

According to traditional logic books, 'All men are mortal' has not only a contradictory, but also a contrary, namely, 'No men are mortal'. This goes over into Frege's symbolism as

$$(x)\ (x \text{ is a man} \rightarrow \neg(x \text{ is mortal})).$$

that is, whatever *x* may be, if *x* is a man *x* is not mortal.

The contradictory of this, in turn, is 'some men are mortal' and this is symbolized by once again attaching the negation-sign:

$$\neg(x)\ (x \text{ is a man} \rightarrow \neg(x \text{ is mortal})).$$

'All *F*s are *G*', 'Some *F*s are *G*', 'Some *F*s are not *G*' and 'No *F*s are *G*' were the patterns of proposition which occurred in the 'square of opposition' of the traditional logic, and which were important for the evaluation of syllogistic arguments. Frege's translations of these patterns enabled him to formalize the logic of syllogisms and of the square of opposition. But he did so within the context of a single and fuller systematization of logic.

Variables which, like the 'x's above, occur within the scope of a quantifier are called by modern logicians 'bound variables'. Variables which occur outside the scope of quantifiers, as in

$$x + y = y + x$$

are called free variables. Frege makes frequent use, both formally and informally, of free variables. In his formal system italic letters are used for free variables, whereas gothic letters are used for bound variables and quantifiers. Frege's explanation of the use of italic letters (CN, p. 132–3) is tantamount to saying that free variables are to be treated as if they were variables bound by a universal quantifier whose scope is the whole expression. With this convention that the scope of a free variable is the whole expression, the possible ambiguity between two kinds of negation (illustrated in the previous chapter and disambiguated there by the positioning of the universal quantifier) is removed. For a free variable allows us only to express the generality of a negation, and not the negation of a generality (see BLA, p. 66). For the negation of a generality we need the quantifier notation; where such negation is not in question, the use of free variables permits the abbreviation of formulae (CN, p. 132).

In *Concept Script* Frege presents a system of logic which is *axiomatic*. Many people who have done school geometry have met the concept of an axiomatic system: a system in which a large number of propositions, called 'theorems', are proved by being derived in a formal manner from a small number of unproved propositions called 'axioms'. Geometry had been axiomatized since the time of Euclid; but logic was not axiomatized before Frege. He sets out the essential elements for its axiomatization in the chapter called 'Representation and derivation of some judgements of pure thought'.

Some principles of logic correspond to the rules which Frege laid out for the use of his symbolism. Such principles, Frege observed, cannot be expressed in his symbolism, since they are presupposed by it. But there are innumerable logical laws which can be stated in it, and the object of the axiomatization is to show that a small kernel of laws can be isolated which potentially entail all the others. More than one way can be found of reducing logic to a small set of principles. Frege proposes a system in which there are nine basic axioms. The first three axioms contain, in addition to the variable letters, only the sign for conditionality, while the next three also contain the negation-sign. Then two axioms introduce the sign for identity of content; and there is an axiom which concerns the sign of generality, the universal quantifier.

In order to set out his propositions Frege needs propositional variables in addition to the primitive truth-functions, that is, letters for which sentences can be substituted. I shall use the letters p, q, r for these variables. Strictly, we need a rule to tell us how to make substitutions for variables. Frege does not enunciate an explicit substitution rule for propositional variables, though there would be no difficulty in formulating one which would accord with his practice.[1]

The three axioms which are the easiest to understand on first acquaintance are those which involve both negation and conditionality. Accordingly, in what follows, I have renumbered Frege's first six axioms.

(1) $(q \rightarrow p) \rightarrow (\neg p \rightarrow \neg q),$

(2) $\neg \neg p \rightarrow p,$

(3) $p \rightarrow \neg \neg p,$

1. Frege himself uses as propositional variables italic letters from the beginning of the alphabet, a, b, c. He uses the same letters in later axioms as individual variables, replaceable by names. In his later writings, but not in the *Concept Script*, this practice was justified by his mature theory that sentences were themselves names.

Any proposition obtained by uniform substitution for the variable letters in these axioms will be something that can be quite naturally described as a self-evident truth. Note that (2) and (3) capture the cancelling-out effect of double negation (CN, p. 156), and an instance of (1) would be 'If it is the case that if he is alive then he is breathing, then if he is not breathing he is not alive' (CN, p. 155).

The axioms which contain only the conditional sign are less easy to grasp intuitively, though if one attends to the definition of the sign, it is possible to see that they too encapsulate logical truisms:

(4) $$p \to (q \to p),$$
(5) $$[r \to (q \to p)] \to [(r \to q) \to (r \to p)],$$
(6) $$[r \to (q \to p)] \to [q \to (r \to p)].$$

Frege tells us that (4) amounts to saying that if a proposition p holds then it also holds in case an arbitrary proposition q holds. He compares (5) to saying 'if a proposition is the necessary consequence of two propositions, and if the first of those two is a necessary consequence of the other, then the original proposition is the necessary consequence of the last proposition alone' (CN, p. 139). This is helpful in enabling us to grasp the structure of the axiom given in (5), but of course it is not equivalent to it, because '$\to$' corresponds to the truth-functional 'if', and not to any notion of necessary consequence. As Frege has earlier emphasized, the assertion of '$p \to q$' simply asserts that it is not the case that 'p' is true and 'q' is false; it does not mean that 'q' follows from 'p'. The same qualification must be made about Frege's gloss on the axiom given by (6): 'if a proposition is the consequence of two conditions, their order is immaterial' (CN, p. 147).

If an axiomatic system is to enable theorems to be deduced from a kernel of axioms, as Frege wished, then the system must contain not only the axioms, or initial formulae, but also rules of inference which enable us to derive one formula from another. Traditional logic contained many rules or laws of inference: for instance, the law of contraposition: 'From "If p, then q" infer "If not q, then not p"' – a law which clearly bears a relationship to the logical truth encapsulated in the first of the axioms to be listed above.

One of the traditional modes of inference was known as *modus ponens*: 'from "p" and from "if p then q" infer "q".' Frege offered, in his symbolic system, to prove all the laws of logic using this as the single rule of inference (CN, p. 119). He acknowledges that other logicians, following Aristotle, employ a whole series of modes of inference; but since it is possible to manage with a single mode, he claims, perspicuity demands that we do so; otherwise there would be no reason to stop with the Aristotelian modes and we could go on adding new ones indefinitely. The other modes of inference will be justified either by particular axioms or by theorems proved from Frege's axioms. Thus, the inference (traditionally called contraposition) from

> If Michael is alive, Michael is breathing

to

> If Michael is not breathing, Michael is not alive

is justified by the axiom given by (1) (CN, p. 154).

To illustrate Frege's procedure, I will show his method of proving the very first theorem which he deduces from his axioms of conditionality. This theorem, let us call it theorem 1, runs as follows:

$$(q \to p) \to \{[r \to (q \to p)] \to [(r \to q) \to (r \to p)]\}.$$

It is derived as follows. Frege starts with his axiom 1, that is, with (4),

$$p \to (q \to p).$$

Then he substitutes his axiom 2, that is, (5), for 'p' in this, so that we get

$$\text{axiom } 2 \to (q \to \text{axiom } 2).$$

Next, he substitutes '$(q \to p)$' for q in this axiom, which gives us

$$\text{axiom } 2 \to [(q \to p) \to \text{axiom } 2];$$

when written out in full in his symbolism this is:

$$\{[r \to (q \to p)] \to [(r \to q) \to (r \to p)]\} \to ((q \to p) \to \\ \{[r \to (q \to p)] \to [(r \to q) \to (r \to p)]\}).$$

By virtue of the rule 'From "p" and from "$p \to q$" infer "q",' we can now derive the theorem from Frege's axioms 1 and 2. For the formula just printed is an instance of axiom 1, and it is itself of the following form

$$\text{axiom } 2 \to \text{theorem } 1.$$

This is something which readers, with some degree of attention, can verify for themselves. But the elaborate nature of even this first proof cast a light on the special meaning which Frege gave to 'perspicuity' when he said that the use of only a single mode of inference was demanded by perspicuity.

Later logicians, following in the footsteps of Frege, have produced formulations of logic which are far easier for the average reader to take in and employ, and Frege's own formulation is now of only historical interest. His claim to be using only one rule of inference is not in fact correct: as already pointed out, and as the proof illustrated above shows, he is not only using *modus ponens* but is tacitly employing another rule which allows us to derive from a given formula a new formula by uniformly substituting any other correctly constructed formula for the variable letters in the original formula. This is no great defect in his system, however, for reduction of the rules of inference to a single rule does not have the unique merits he claims.

What is important is that his first six axioms are in fact sufficient for the derivation of all laws of logic which do not involve breaking up propositions into function and argument, but which treat them as whole units. (Indeed, they are more than sufficient for this purpose, because it turns out that some of the axioms can be proved from others.[2]) This branch of logic is now called the propositional calculus, in contrast to the predicate calculus or functional calculus which takes into account the manner in which propositions are constructed out of their parts.

In order to follow Frege's method of dealing with the functional calculus, we have to go beyond his first six axioms. The seventh and eighth axioms contain his symbol for identity of content:

(7) $$(c \equiv d) \rightarrow [f(c) \rightarrow f(d)],$$
(8) $$c \equiv c.$$

Axiom 7, Frege explains, says that we may replace 'c' everywhere by 'd' if $c \equiv d$. While axiom 8, he says, states that the content of c is identical with the content of c.

From axioms 7 and 8 Frege proves, by simple steps, a number of other theorems about identity of content, for instance

$$(c \equiv d) \rightarrow (d \equiv c).$$

Axiom 9 is the one that is crucial for the development of the functional calculus. In our modernized version of Frege's symbolism it runs as follows

(9) $$(x)\,(fx) \rightarrow fc.$$

This is tantamount to saying that if fx holds generally, then it holds of any given object. The example that Frege gives to illustrate it is:

If whatever is a bird can fly, then if this ostrich is a bird it can fly,

and from this we can, in due course, derive

If this ostrich is a bird and cannot fly then some birds cannot fly.

---

2. See W. and M. Kneale, *The Development of Logic*, Oxford University Press, 1962, pp. 490–91.

In addition to this axiom, axiom 9, in developing the functional calculus Frege makes use of two rules which he had stated when introducing the quantifier notation.

The first rule is that from $\Phi(c)$ we may infer $(x)\,\Phi\,(x)$ provided that c occurs only in the argument places of $\Phi(\ )$, and provided that (x) does not already occur within $\Phi(c)$ (CN, p. 132). (The second provision is necessary to prevent a variable in the original expression falling within the scope of the newly introduced quantifier.)

This rule seems puzzling: is it a licence to make an inference from 'this is an ostrich' to 'everything is an ostrich'? To dissolve the puzzlement we must first realize that this is not an axiom or theorem formalizing a logical truth like that expressed in axiom 9. It is a formal rule for the transition from one thesis to another within Frege's particular system: and the rest of that system is so designed so that we will never reach a point within it where we are licensed to assert '$\Phi(c)$' without this having itself been derived in such a way as to make the generalization sound. (It may perhaps be compared with a rule such as 'always take the second turn to the right', which could be sound within a particular maze, but unsound as a general rule for finding one's way out of any maze.)

The second rule is that from '$p \rightarrow \Phi(c)$' we can derive '$p \rightarrow (x)\Phi(x)$', provided that p is an expression in which c does not occur, and c stands only in argument places of $\Phi(c)$. Frege justified this by saying that if '$(x)\,\Phi\,(x)$' is false, it must be possible to supply a meaning for '$\Phi(c)$' which brings it out false; but since it is the case that $p \rightarrow \Phi(c)$ this will not be possible, for this formula means that, whatever c may be, the case in which $\Phi(c)$ would be denied and p affirmed does not occur. The justification clearly depends on Frege's convention that an italic letter has for its scope the entire judgement in which it occurs.[3]

---

3. See p. 40. This convention is explicitly stated at the point in *Concept Script* where the two rules are introduced (CN, p. 132–3). The residual puzzling feature of the introduction of the rules is that at the point where the axiom of quantification theory is introduced (CN, p. 163) Frege says: 'Let b mean an

Frege's ninth axiom, plus these two rules, in conjunction with the rules and axioms for propositional calculus, suffices for the derivation of all truths of the functional calculus.

The third part of *Concept Script* is entitled 'Some topics from a general theory of series'. It is intended to give samples of the way in which his concept script can be used for the exact formulation of arithmetic. One further piece of notation is introduced at the beginning of the third part: a notation to permit the introduction of abbreviations by definition. '⊩—$A \equiv B$' serves to lay down a definition, with the new symbol, or definiendum, occupying the place of 'B' and the symbolic expression it abbreviates occupying the place of 'A'. The expression begins with two vertical strokes, not the single vertical judgement stroke, because, as Frege says, the sentence does not say 'The right side of the equation has the same content as the left side', but 'They are to have the same content'. Nothing follows from the definition which could not be established without it; its function is solely to simplify proofs (CN, p. 168).

Though a definition is not a judgement, Frege says, it is easily converted into one; once the definition has been accepted it becomes an analytic proposition, true in virtue of the definition itself. It is this dual role, Frege says, which is indicated by the doubling of the judgement stroke. The purpose to which Frege first puts his definition sign is to define a notion of the *hereditariness* of a property. He introduces a new sign which, he tells us, is meant to be equivalent to

The property F is hereditary in the f-series.

This sign is declared by his formal definition to be equivalent to

$$(y)\,(F(y) \to (x)\,(f(y,x) \to F(x)).$$

What is a hereditary property, and why is Frege interested in

---

ostrich; that is, an individual animal belonging to this species.' Here, an italic letter is being used not as a free variable but as a dummy name of an individual.

defining the notion? To assist us in understanding the answer to the first question, Frege proposes the following instance of the defining formula:

(y) (if y is human, then (x) (if x is a child of y, x is human).)

This tells us that the property of being human is a hereditary property – hereditary in the series generated by the relation *child of*. The answer to the second question is that Frege wishes to use the notion of a hereditary property in order to define the general notion of following in a series. This in turn can be used to give a purely logical account of the relation of succession which links the numbers in the number series.

The relation of following in a series which Frege defined is often now called 'the ancestral relation', since one instance of it is the relation of an ancestor to his descendants. A is an ancestor of B if B is a child of A, or a child of a child of A, or a child of a child of a child of A, and so on. What Frege wanted to do was to give an exact logical formula to capture the intuitive understanding of ordering in a series which is expressed by 'and so on'. To do so he proposed the following definition:

B follows A in the f-series

is to mean the same as

For all F, if whatever has the relation f to A has the property F, and if F is hereditary in the f-series, then B has the property F.

Thus, if the f-series is the series generated by the relation *child of*, then B will follow A in the series (will be a descendant of A) if B has all the hereditary properties which belong to all the children of A.

Frege proves several theorems which follow from his definitions. One of the most interesting is this:

If A has a property F which is hereditary in the f-series and if B follows A in the f-series, then y has the property F.

Applied to the number series, this theorem can be used as a

basis for mathematical induction, the procedure by which we conclude that if a property belongs to the number 0, and belongs to any number which is the successor of any number to which it belongs, than it belongs to all natural numbers. The application of the definitions of *Concept Script* to the development of the natural number series had to wait, however, for the publication some years later of *The Foundations of Arithmetic*.

CHAPTER 4

THE FOUNDATIONS OF ARITHMETIC, I

Frege was led to write *The Foundations of Arithmetic* by a conviction that the most fundamental concepts and operations of arithmetic were ill understood by the best mathematicians and philosophers of his day. Our insight into the basic structure of arithmetic, he claims, is scandalously defective. No one can even give a coherent answer to the question of what the number one is, or what the numeral 'one' signifies. To bring this out he imagines the following dialogue.

A. What is the number one?
B. It is a thing.
A. But what thing?
B. Anything you like.
A. So in an equation I can replace '1' with whatever I like?
B. Just as in '$x + x - x = x$' you can replace x with any number.
A. In '$1 + 1 = 2$' can we replace '1' with 'the Moon'?

At this point there seems no answer for B to make. If we put 'the Moon' in place of '1' both times, we seem to produce a falsehood: there is only one Moon circling the Earth, not two. On the other hand, if we put something else in the second place, say 'the Sun', we are doing exactly what we would not be allowed to do in B's parallel case. The algebraic formula expresses a truth only if we always substitute the same numeral for the same letter.

In fact, Frege argues, it is wrong to think that statements about numbers are generalizations about non-numerical objects in the way that algebraic formulae can be regarded as general statements about numbers. So, '1 × 1 = 1', he insists, 'says nothing about the Moon, nothing about the Sun, nothing about the Sahara, nothing about the Peak of Tenerife.' Rather, the number one, *prima facie* at least, is itself a particular object, which has properties all its own, such as that of remaining unchanged when multiplied by itself. But the nature of this object, and of the other positive integers, remains totally obscure, while most people are not even aware that there is a problem here.

If the nature of numbers is poorly understood, the nature of calculation also is generally misconceived. It is sometimes regarded as a special kind of thought: 'aggregative mechanical thought' was a definition offered by one of Frege's contemporaries. But, according to Frege, thought is essentially the same everywhere: there are not different laws of thought to suit the different kinds of objects that we think about. The major purpose of his book is to argue that all inferences which appear to be peculiar to mathematics (such as, for instance, mathematical induction) are based on general laws of logic.

Frege's task involved both mathematical and philosophical considerations: and he was aware that many of the mathematicians of his day were suspicious of philosophy. The reason for this, Frege maintains, is a damaging confusion within philosophy itself – a failure to distinguish the realm of logic from the realm of psychology. Psychology was – he agreed – no concern of the pure mathematician: but logic, rightly understood, was something quite different from psychology.

Psychology is the experimental study of the mind, the pursuit of regularities governing mental phenomena. In Frege's day it enjoyed a particular prestige among those philosophers who belonged to the empiricist school, that is to say, among those philosophers who sought to account for all human knowledge on the basis of sensory experience. For thoroughgoing empiricists, the contents of the human mind are reducible to two main classes. On the one hand there are sense-impressions, including both deliverances of the outer senses and inner sensations and feelings, and on the other hand there are mental images, formed from traces of earlier sense-impressions. The best known empiricist philosopher of the nineteenth century was John Stuart Mill, and Frege devotes substantial sections of his book to the refutation of Mill's account of number. Already in his introduction he insists that sensations and mental images have nothing to do with arithmetic. 'The fluctuation and indeterminacy typical of these items of consciousness stands in sharp contrast to the determinacy and stability of the concepts and objects of mathematics.'(FA pp. v–vi.)

Frege does not, of course, deny that a mathematician has sensations and mental images, or that mental images may play a part in the thought processes of someone who is carrying out an arithmetical calculation. But he offers two arguments to show that images and thoughts in our mind are not what arithmetic is about. First of all, different mathematicians associate different images with the same number: one person may think of the word 'hundred', another may think of the symbol '100', another of the letter 'C': this shows that images are something merely accessory to arithmetic. Secondly, even if psychology were to progress beyond the study of images to the study of the thoughts in our mind, it would still have nothing to contribute to arithmetic. Suppose psychology could give causal explanations of the occurrence of the thought that ten squared is one hundred, for instance. Even so, psychology would be totally different from arithmetic. For arithmetic is concerned with the truth of such propositions; psychology is concerned only with their occurrence in thought. 'A proposition may be thought, and again may be true; let us never confuse these two things.'(FA, p. vi.)

A proposition may be thought of, without being true: as when someone makes a mistake in multiplication, and comes up with an erroneous product. He has the thought that $125 \times 387 = 48\,357$, but there is no such arithmetical truth. Again, a proposition may be true, without being thought of: Pythagoras' theorem held long before Pythagoras proved it. 'A proposition no more ceases to be true when I stop thinking of it than the sun ceases to exist when I shut my eyes.' (FA, p. vi.)

Psychology is interested in the causal conditions of our mental processes; mathematics is interested in the proof, or justification, of the thoughts we think. But cause and proof are quite different things. Without an appropriate ration of phosphorus in his brain, no doubt, Pythagoras would have been unable to carry through the proof of his theorem; but that does not mean that a statement of the phosphorus content of his brain should occur as a line in the proof.

If human bodies and human brains have evolved, no doubt there has also been evolution in human consciousness. So if mathematics is about sensations and ideas, mathematicians should be cautious about making very general claims. When an astronomer draws conclusions about epochs very distant in the past we would be entitled to reproach him thus:

'You reckon that $2 \times 2 = 4$: but the idea of number has a history, an evolution. It may be doubted whether it had yet progressed so far. How do you know that in that distant past that proposition already existed? Might not the creatures then alive have held the proposition $2 \times 2 = 5$? Perhaps it was only later that natural selection, in the struggle for existence, evolved the proposition $2 \times 2 = 4$, and perhaps that in its turn is destined to develop into $2 \times 2 = 3$.' (FA, pp. vi–vii.)

Frege's *reductio ad absurdum* succeeds in its object of showing that arithmetic cannot be regarded as a science whose object is human sensation and imagination. But it is important to be clear exactly what he is refuting. Here, as he does more systematically elsewhere, Frege draws a distinction between ideas and concepts. Ideas are the mental images and other mental phenomena which are the subject matter of psychology: these are, perhaps, subject to the operation of evolution but they are irrelevant to arithmetic. Concepts, on the other hand, are an object of study for the mathematician; but concepts are not things that evolve. It is wrong to think of them as sprouting and growing in the individual mind. If concepts have a history it is not a history of their own development, but only of our discovery and expression of them. What Frege meant by 'concept' is already partly known to readers who have followed the account of his *Concept Script*; a fuller account will be given when we come to consider his later writings. What is clear at all periods of his life is that a concept is something very different from a mental image, and that it is meant to be something objective, not subjective.

Mathematics, therefore, must be strictly separated from psychology. The reluctance of mathematicians to cooperate with philosophers was understandable at a time when philosophy itself was not sharply distinguished from experimental psychology. But while mathematics must be freed from any connection with psychology it must, in Frege's view, forge closer links with logic. It is not just that any inquiry into the cogency of a proof must be a matter of logic: that everyone will admit. We must go further and ensure that every definition which is used in mathematics is itself justified with the same rigour as is used in formal proofs. It is not sufficient to assume that a definition is justified if it is fruitful in use and if no contradictions have been discovered as a result of its employment. To justify definitions in the appropriate way it is necessary to go into the general logical foundations of mathematics to an unprecedented depth.

Frege concludes the introduction to the *Foundations* by stating three fundamental principles governing the work. These are as follows.

(1) A sharp distinction must be made between what is logical and what is psychological, what is subjective and what is objective.

(2) We must not ask for the meaning of a word in isolation, but only in the context of a proposition.

(3) Attention must always be paid to the distinction between concept and object.

The first principle is a summary of what has gone before, but the second two come as something of a surprise, and indeed their meaning is not at this stage clear. Frege links the second principle to the first, by saying that if we do not attend to it, we will be almost forced to take mental pictures as meanings of words. What he seems to mean is that if we come across a word in a proposition which does not seem to correspond to an object in the external world, we may be tempted to say that it means some inner object, a subjective mental item. The relevance of this to arithmetic will become clear only later, as will the importance of the distinction between concept and object. It will be best to postpone the discussion of Frege's 'fundamental principles' until we have considered the main lines of the book, after which we will be in a better position to see in what ways he has made use of them.

Almost half of Frege's book is taken up with discussing, and refuting, the views of other philosophers and mathematicians. While he is discussing the opinions of others, some of his own insights are artfully insinuated, and this makes easier the eventual presentation of his own theory. But the main purpose of the lengthy polemic is to convince readers of the seriousness of the problems to which he will later offer solutions. Without this preamble, as he says, we would lack the first prerequisite for learning anything: namely, the knowledge of our own ignorance (FA, p. iii).

The survey of opposing views is divided into three parts devoted to different, but related topics: the nature of arithmetical propositions, the concept of number and the notion of one or unity.

The question about the nature of arithmetical propositions is put by Frege in the following way: Are they a priori or a posteriori? Synthetic or analytic? Here Frege is using terms which were given widespread currency in the previous century by Immanuel Kant.

According to Kant the distinction between a priori and a posteriori is primarily a distinction between modes of knowledge: we know a truth a priori if we know it independently of all experience; we know it a posteriori if we know it through experience. The distinction between analytic and synthetic, on the other hand, is a distinction made by Kant in terms of judgements, and in particular in terms of subject–predicate judgements. The judgement that A is B is analytic if the predicate B belongs to the subject A as something which is contained in the concept A, otherwise it is synthetic. Because the two distinctions are drawn in different terms – one in terms of epistemology, the other in terms of logic – we cannot assume that they coincide, so that, for instance, we cannot assume all a priori propositions are analytic and and all synthetic propositions are a posteriori. Kant himself believed that the two distinctions did not coincide: he maintained that there were such things as synthetic a priori judgements, and that these had an extremely important place in any account of human knowledge.

Frege adapts Kant's distinctions to his own purpose. To ensure that talk of 'a priori knowledge' involves no confusion between psychology and logic, he reminds us that it is possible to discover the content of a proposition before we hit on a proof of it, so we must distinguish between how we first come to believe it and how we would eventually justify it. The Kantian distinctions, as he presents them, concern not the content of the judgement, nor the method of arriving at it, but its justification (FA, p. 3).

First let us note that there must *be* a justification, if we are to talk of knowledge at all (whether a priori or a posteriori). For, traditionally, the difference between knowledge and mere belief is that knowledge is belief which is both true and justified. To talk of an a priori mistake, Frege says, is as nonsensical as to talk of a blue concept. For knowing a priori is a mode of knowing, and one can only know what is true.[1]

When a proposition is called a posteriori or analytic in my sense, this is not a judgement about the conditions, psychological, physiological and

---

1. Is Frege denying that one can know a priori that a certain proposition – say $7 + 5 = 13$ – is false? Surely not, but he treats a priori knowledge that p is false as knowledge that the negation of p is true.

physical, which have made it possible to represent the content of the proposition in consciousness. Nor is a judgement about the possibly defective method by which some other person has come to believe it true. Rather, it is a judgement about the fundamental ground which provides the justification for believing it to be true. (FA, p. 3.)

If the proposition is a mathematical one, the justification for it must be mathematical, not psychological. So if we are to settle whether it is analytic or synthetic, we must find its proof and trace it back to primitive truths. If in this process we come only on general logical laws, and definitions whose permissibility is established by such laws, then the truth is analytic; but if the proof involves truths which belong to the sphere of some special science, then the proposition is synthetic. Frege goes on:

For a truth to be a posteriori, its proof must be impossible without appeal to facts, that is to truths which are unprovable and lack generality and contain assertions about particular objects. If, on the other hand, it is possible to construct the proof entirely from general laws, which themselves neither admit nor require proof, then the truth is a priori. (FA, p. 4.)

We have to read this passage carefully if we are to see what, for Frege, is the difference between the a priori/a posteriori distinction and the analytic/synthetic distinction. It is no longer a matter of epistemology versus logic: it is a matter of degree of generality. A truth is a priori if it is provable from general laws, without appeal to particular facts; a truth is not only a priori, but also analytic, if the general laws from which it is provable are general laws of *logic*. A law is a law of logic if it is universally applicable and not restricted to particular disciplines.

Later in the *Foundations* (p. 101), Frege allied himself with Kant in stating that the truths of geometry are synthetic and a priori. This thesis enables us to see more clearly how he understands the distinctions between the a priori and the analytic. Geometry is a priori, because geometrical theorems are provable from general laws (for example, from the axioms of Euclid) and make no appeal to any particular lines, figures or solid bodies. But geometry is not analytic, because its axioms involve spatial concepts; and these concepts are not applicable in all disciplines, since not everything we can think about is spatial. As non-Euclidean geometries show, some of the geometrical axioms can be denied without self-contradiction. This, Frege says, 'shows that the axioms of geometry are independent of one another and of the primitive laws of logic and consequently are synthetic' (FA, p. 21).

The great question to which Frege addresses himself is whether arithmetic, like geometry, depends upon specific non-logical laws, or whether it can be proved purely from general laws of logic. This question can be satisfactorily answered only if arithmetic, like geometry, can be successfully axiomatized, that is to say, if all its truths can be shown to depend on a handful of primitive truths. When this has been done, it will be possible to see whether these truths are all of a general, logical, kind, or whether some of them contain concepts which are irreducible and peculiar to arithmetic.

Perhaps the concept of number will turn out to have a role in arithmetic similar to that which spatial concepts have in geometry. Or perhaps – and this is the hope which Frege holds out – the numbers themselves (the cardinal numbers such as one, two, three, and so on) will turn out to be definable in purely logical terms. In the former case, truths of arithmetic will be synthetic; in the latter case, they will be analytic.

Well, can arithmetic be axiomatized? Can, for instance, the formulae

$$7 + 5 = 12$$
$$135\,664 + 37\,863 = 173\,527$$

and infinitely many other similar sums be reduced to a handful of self-evident truths? Frege takes it for granted that if axiomatization is to be possible, the set of primitive truths must be small enough to be easily surveyable. Can the infinity of truths of arithmetic be reduced to a manageable group?

Reduction is only possible if the individual numbers occurring in the formulae can be defined away. Leibniz, long ago, had given a hint how this might be done, in a passage which Frege quotes from *Nouveaux Essais*.

> It is not an immediate truth that 2 and 2 are 4; provided it be granted that 4 signifies 3 and 1. It can be proved, as follows:
> Definitions: (1) 2 is 1 and 1
> (2) 3 is 2 and 1
> (3) 4 is 3 and 1
> Axiom: If equals be substituted for equals, the equality remains.
> Proofs: $2 + 2 = 2 + 1 + 1$ (by Def. 1) $= 3 + 1$ (by Def. 2) $= 4$ (by Def. 3.)
> Therefore, $2 + 2 = 4$ (by the Axiom).

Frege points out that the proof makes a tacit appeal to the axiom $a + (b + c) = (a + b) + c$, which is concealed by the lack of parentheses. But if we add this axiom, Frege maintains, we can see easily that a proof similar to Leibniz's can be given for every formula of addition. 'Every number, that means, is to be defined in terms of its predecessor ... Through such definitions we reduce the whole infinite set of numbers to the number one and increase by one, and every one of the infinitely many numerical formulae can be proved from a few general propositions.' (FA, p. 8.)

Later in *Foundations* Frege sets out in detail how this programme is to be carried out. But first, he makes a contrast between this Leibnizian view which he adopts and the views of other equally distinguished philosophers which would involve an outright rejection of the programme of axiomatization.

The opposition comes from two contrasting quarters, rationalist and empiricist. Kant regarded each arithmetical formula as an irreducible synthetic truth, known a priori by intuition. John Stuart Mill agreed with Kant that arithmetic was synthetic, but he thought it was a posteriori: definitions of individual numbers in the style of Leibniz presupposed particular matters of fact, discovered by experience. Frege shows that neither of these positions is tenable.

Kant claims that each arithmetical proposition is known by

intuition. In adding together 7 and 5, he says, we 'call to our aid the intuition corresponding to one of them, say our five fingers'. 'Intuition' seems to mean the use of the imagination – for if intuition involved any appeal to experience, then arithmetic would be empirical rather than a priori. But do we really have an intuition of 37 863 fingers? Or of 135 664 fingers? And if we did, would not the value of 135 664 + 37 863 be immediately obvious, without needing to be worked out?

Perhaps Kant meant his thesis to apply only to small numbers. But even in the case of ten fingers, many different images come to mind, depending on the positioning of the fingers. And how can we make a fundamental distinction between small and large numbers? If formulae involving numbers above ten are provable, why not formulae involving smaller numbers?

Frege turns his attention from Kant to Mill. Mill had claimed in his *A System of Logic* (SL) that the definition of each number involved the assertion of a physical fact.

Each of the numbers two, three, four &c., denotes physical phenomena, and connotes a physical property of those phenomena. Two, for instance, denotes all pairs of things, and twelve all dozens of things, connoting what makes them pairs or dozens: and that which makes them so is something physical; since it cannot be denied that two apples are physically distinguishable from three apples, two horses from one horse, and so forth: that they are a different visible and tangible phenomenon. (SL, III, 24, 5.)

Mill has some difficulty in making clear exactly what the physical property is which is connoted by the name of a number, and he has to agree that the senses cannot so easily distinguish between a hundred and two horses and a hundred and three as they can between two horses and three. But he concludes that the property which is connoted by the names of the numbers like three and four is:

some property belonging to the agglomeration of things which we call by the name; and that property is the characteristic manner in which the agglomeration is made up of, and may be separated into, parts. (SL,III, 24, 5.)

He illustrates this property in the case of the number three by saying:

Collections of objects exist, which while they impress the senses thus, ∴ may be separated into two parts thus ∙∙∙. This proposition being granted, we term all such parcels Threes. (SL, II, 6, 2.)

What a mercy, Frege comments, that not everything in the world is nailed down; for if it were we should not be able to separate the parts, and two and one would not be three!

Objections can be made to Mill's proposal which are closely parallel to those against Kant's proposals. We cannot point to any physical fact asserted in the definition of the number 777 864, any more than we can point to an intuition of such a number. On Mill's view, someone who can calculate with nine-figure numbers would have to be credited with an astonishing knowledge of physics; just as on Kant's view such a person would have to be endowed with an extraordinarily vivid imagination. Mill is no more entitled than Kant to claim that large numbers have to be treated differently from small: if we can form 11 from 10 and 1 simply by definition, without having seen the corresponding collection of objects, there is no reason why we should not similarly construct two out of 1 and 1.

Both Kant and Mill explain number by appeal to features of aggregates; the only difference being that Mill is thinking of actual vision, and Kant of the visual imagination. But such an approach fails to take account of the universal applicability of number. If it was taken literally, it would mean that it was incorrect to speak of three peals of a bell, or three methods of solving an equation.

Neither Kant nor Mill provides a serious alternative to the Leibnizian programme of establishing arithmetical truths by deriving them, via definitions, from a few initial propositions. But even if we adopt this programme, the questions will remain whether the initial propositions (and, along with them, the theorems provable from them) are a posteriori or a priori, and whether they are analytic or synthetic. Mill might be wrong in rejecting the construction of numbers by definition, and yet correct in maintaining that arithmetic is essentially an empirical science.

Mill claims, for instance, that a principle such as 'the sums of equals are equals' is an inductive truth or law of nature of the highest order. Inductive truths are generalizations based on individual instances. Assertions of such truths, according to Mill, must always be to some extent tentative or hypothetical. But surely 'the sums of equals are equals' is something which is categorically certain: how then can it be an inductive truth?

Mill maintains that the principle contains a hypothetical element: that is to say, it makes the assumption that all numbers involved are numbers of the same or of equal units.

[T]his is never accurately true, for one actual pound weight is not exactly equal to another, nor one measured mile's length to another; a nicer balance, or more accurate measuring instruments, would always detect some difference. (SL, II, 6, 3.)

Frege objects that Mill is here confusing arithmetic with its applications. If we pour 2 unit volumes of liquid into 5 unit volumes of liquid we shall have 7 unit volumes of liquid. But that is not the meaning of the proposition $5 + 2 = 7$, but an application of it. Moreover, it is a law which only holds good in certain physical circumstances – in the absence, for instance, of a chemical reaction which alters the volume. The pure arithmetical proposition is quite different from the applications which can be made of it, which often are physical propositions and do presuppose observed facts. Arithmetic can be applied to physics, but it cannot be based on physics, because it is applicable to many items other than physical objects.

If arithmetical laws are to be inductive, the instances from which they are to be derived would have to be themselves arithmetical. But we would be moving in a circle if we tried to establish axioms of arithmetic by appeal to individual numerical formulae and to establish individual formulae by appeal to the axioms.

Moreover, the inductive method involves generalization over similar instances. But individual numbers vary greatly from each other: some are odd, some even, some squares, some cubes and so on. How could we make reliable generalizations from such a mixed bag of instances? In making inductions we assume that any position in space or time is the same as any other: two instances will not differ simply because they occur at different times or in different places. But position in the number series is not a matter of indifference like position in space: it is of the nature of numbers to be arranged in a fixed order. Each number is formed in its own way and has its own peculiarities, which, Frege says, are 'specially prominent in the cases of 0, 1 and 2'.

To try to establish arithmetic by induction is to put the cart before the horse. Scientific induction depends upon probability theory. But probability theory could never be developed without presupposing arithmetical laws.

Arithmetic, then, is not an empirical science; it is not a posteriori. But if it is a priori is it synthetic or analytic? Kant maintained that arithmetic, like geometry, is synthetic a priori. But Frege thinks that the similarity between arithmetic and geometry is commonly overestimated. As already remarked, one geometrical point, or line or plane, considered by itself, is indistinguishable from any other; whereas each number has its own peculiarities. Only when several points, or lines or planes are included together in a single intuition can we distinguish them from each other. In geometry, therefore, it is quite intelligible that general propositions should be derived from intuition. And indeed the domain of geometry is precisely the realm of what is spatially intuitable, whether actual or imaginary.

The wildest visions of delirium, the boldest inventions of legend and poetry, where animals speak and stars stand still, where men are turned to stone and trees turn into men, where the drowning haul themselves up out of the swamps by their own topknots – all these remain, so long as they remain intuitable, still subject to the axioms of geometry. Conceptual thought alone can after a fashion shake off this yoke when it assumes, say, a space of four dimensions or positive curvature. To study such conceptions is not useless by any means; but it is to leave the ground of intuition entirely behind. If we do make use of intuition even here, as an aid, it is intuition of Euclidean space, the only space of which we have any picture. Only now the intuition is not taken at its face value, but as symbolic of something else; for example, we call straight or plane what we actually intuit as curved. (FA, p. 20.)

Arithmetic has an even wider domain than geometry, psychology or physics. Physics and psychology deal with the active world of cause and effect (*Wirklichkeit*); geometry deals with the world of the imaginable; arithmetic deals with the world of thought. Everything that is thinkable is also countable; and the laws of number cannot be denied without calling into question the laws of thought. Hence, Frege concludes, the basis of arithmetic lies deeper than any of the sciences, including geometry. He proposes that arithmetical truths are not only a priori, but analytic. The truths of arithmetic are related to the truths of logic in the same way as Euclid's theorems are to his axioms.

This proposal may seem shocking. How can the vast tree of the science of number have its roots in bare identities? Can so rich a content be extracted from the empty husks of logic? As Mill said, 'the doctrine that we can discover facts, detect the hidden processes of nature, by an artful manipulation of language, is so contrary to common sense, that a person must have made some advances in philosophy to believe it' (SL, II, 6, 2).

But someone who maintains, as Frege does, that arithmetic is derivable from logic does not mean that arithmetical truths are truths about mere symbols. The symbols have a content, which is made perceptible through the symbols; but the content of the symbols, he is claiming, is not anything intuitable or perceivable by the senses. This holds for both the truths of arithmetic and the truths of logic; and if the former can indeed be derived from the latter, then 'the prodigious development of arithmetical studies, with their multitudinous applications, will suffice to put an end to the widespread contempt for analytic judgements and to the legend of the sterility of pure logic'.

Frege now turns to a general consideration of the concept of cardinal number. Each individual number, it may well be, can be defined in terms of the number one and the notion of increase by one. But these items must themselves be defined; and in the derivation general propositions will be needed, which must themselves be derived from the general concept of number. What, then, is number?

Is it a property of external things? Number words often appear as adjectives: we speak of three horses or four horses as we speak of black horses and white horses, and this may suggest that number is a property of things in the way that colour is. Again, when we speak of 'four thoroughbred horses' it looks as if 'four' modifies 'thoroughbred horse' in the same way as 'thoroughbred' modifies 'horse' (FA, p. 64).

Can we really class number with properties such as colour and solidity? Colour and solidity are perceptible by the senses; and Mill had argued that number, too, was a property perceptible by the senses. Two apples, he said, are physically different from three apples, and two horses are a different physical and tangible phenomenon from one horse. But we cannot infer from this that twoness or threeness is physical: *one* pair of boots may be the same visible and tangible phenomenon as *two* boots. Moreover, a man may have two horses, one in Germany and one in America; and if these two horses are never brought together they do not form a 'physical and tangible phenomenon' at all.

Mill had claimed that number was a property of an agglomeration of things, a property consisting of 'the characteristic manner in which the agglomeration is made up of, and may be separated into parts'. But there is no *one* characteristic way of separating an agglomeration: a bundle of straw can be separated into parts by cutting all the straws in half, by splitting it up into single straws, or by dividing it into two bundles. Moreover, things do not have to be agglomerated at all in order to be counted. We do not have to hold a rally of all the blind in Germany to attach a sense to the expression 'The number of blind people in Germany'. A thousand grains of wheat, scattered by the sower, are still a thousand grains.

The difficulty in regarding number as a physical property comes out particularly clearly in the case of the number one. The most plausible suggestion made here is that being one amounts to being undivided and being isolated. If that were so, Frege says, then we would expect animals to have an idea of unity: a dog staring at the Moon can see that it is isolated, and can distinguish individual objects such as its master or another dog. But does a dog really have a concept of the number one?

It will notice a difference, no doubt, between being set on by several dogs and being set on by one dog, but this is what Mill calls the physical difference. The question at issue is: is the dog conscious, however dimly, of that common element expressed by the word 'one' in different cases such as when it is bitten by one larger dog and when it chases one cat? This seems to me unlikely. (FA, p. 42.)

Properties such as being undivided, or being isolated, which animals perceive no less than we do, cannot be what is essential to the mathematical concept of unity.

Frege's arguments against Mill are successful in showing that number is not a physical or tangible property, whether of things or agglomerations of things. But they seem to leave open the possibility that number might be some other kind of property of things, even if it is not a property which is perceptible by the senses.

It is true, as Frege says, that number differs from a property like colour or solidity by being applicable over a far wider range. As he said later, summarizing the argument here presented, 'we can count just about everything that can be an object of thought: the ideal as well as the real, concepts as well as objects, temporal as well as spatial entities, events as well as bodies, methods as well as theorems' (CP, p. 112). But this does not seem a very convincing argument to show that number is not a property of things. Why should there not be some properties which apply to many different kinds of things? Frege uses it as an argument against regarding 'one' as a word for a property that it would be remarkable that every single thing should possess this property.

It would be incomprehensible why we should still ascribe it expressly to a thing at all. It is only in virtue of the possibility of something not being wise that it makes sense to say 'Solon is wise'. The content of a concept diminishes as its extension increases; if its extension becomes all-embracing, its content must vanish altogether. (FA, p. 40.)

This passage is difficult to reconcile with some of the things Frege says elsewhere about the nature of concepts. He is himself prepared to consider *being identical with oneself* a property (cf. FA, p. 87). If this is a property, surely it is one which applies quite universally: everything is identical with itself. Neither in the case of 'one', then, nor in the case of the other numbers does the range of applicability seem to establish that number is not a property.

But Frege has other and better arguments to bring out the difference between numbers and properties such as colour. We speak of a tree as having 1000 leaves and as having green leaves; but there is this difference, that each leaf is green, whereas each leaf is not 1000. The leaves, collectively, form the foliage of the tree; the foliage, like the leaves, is green, but again the foliage is not 1000. So 1000, considered as a property, seems to belong neither to any single leaf nor to the totality of them all.

If I give someone a stone and tell him to find its weight, he knows precisely what he is to investigate. But if I give him a pile of playing-cards and ask him to find their number, he needs to know whether I want to know the number of cards, or of packs of cards, or suits. Colour belongs to a surface independently of any choice of ours; but the number 2 or 104 does not belong to the pile of cards in its own right, but in view of the way we have chosen to regard it.

What we choose to call a complete pack is obviously an arbitrary decision, in which the pile of playing cards has no say. But it is when we examine the pile in the light of this decision, that we discover perhaps that we can call it two complete packs. Anyone who did not know what we call a complete pack would probably discover in the pile any number you like before hitting on two. (FA, p. 29.)

While I cannot alter the colour of a thing by thinking of it differently, I can think of the *Iliad* as one poem, or as 24 books, or as 115 477 words. Frege quotes from Berkeley's *Essay Towards a New Theory of Vision*: 'According as the mind variously combines its ideas, the unit varies; and as the unit, so the number, which is only a collection of units, doth also vary. We call a window one, a chimney one, and yet a house in which there are many windows, and many chimneys, hath an equal right to be called one, and many houses go to the making of one city.'

If number is not a property of things, does that mean that it is something subjective, a product of mental processes? If so, it would belong to the subject matter of psychology; and this is something which Frege vigorously rejected. From the fact that the number to be attached to something in the world will depend on a prior decision of ours, it is quite wrong to conclude that number is not an objective matter. Number is no more a product of mental processes than the North Sea is. It is a matter of our arbitrary choice which tract of water to call 'The North Sea'; but that does not make the North Sea belong to psychology rather than to geography.

If we say 'The North Sea is 10 000 square miles in extent' then neither by 'North Sea' nor by '10 000' do we refer to any state of or process in our minds: on the contrary we assert something quite objective, which is independent of our ideas and everything of the sort. (FA, p. 34.)

Something can be objective, in Frege's sense, without being tangible, or spatial, or causally operative. The axis of the Earth and the equator are objective, but they are not tangible objects.

Numbers and colours are both alike objective, but only colours are perceptible by the senses.

The idea that numbers are something subjective, like a mental image, leads to absurd results. Mental images are private in the sense that my mental images are not your mental images, and your mental images are not mine. If the number two were something like a mental image, then it would have to be private to individuals.

We should then have it might be many millions of twos on our hands. We should have to speak of my two and your two, of one two and all twos ... As new generations of children grew up, new generations of twos would continually be being born, and in the course of millennia these might evolve, for all we could tell, to such a pitch that two of them would make five. (FA, p. 37.)

And many numerals might turn out to be empty symbols. How can we be sure, for instance, that there exists in some mind somewhere an image corresponding to the symbol for ten to the tenth? 'It would be strange', Frege concludes, 'if the most exact of all the sciences had to seek support from psychology, which is still feeling its way none too surely.'

Frege now turns to consider the suggestion that a number is a set. He observes that if 'set' is taken as equivalent to 'multitude' or 'plurality', then such a definition would not cover the numbers 0 and 1. 'The word "set"', he observes, 'easily evokes the thought of a heap of things in space, as is evident from the expression "set of dishes"; and thus, like J.S. Mill, one very easily retains the childlike conception of a number itself as a heap or aggregate.' (CP, p. 114.) However, it will turn out later that in Frege's own view a number is rather like a set, so the proposal is not one which can be dismissed out of hand.

The first question is: What is it that a number is a set *of*? The traditional answer to this question, first given by Euclid, is that a number is a set of units. We need, then, to enquire what is a unit. Is 'unit' a synonym for 'thing', if any and every thing is a unit or can be regarded as one?

Frege says that an answer popular among philosophers is that when we describe two items to be counted as 'units' we are ascribing to them a certain identity with each other. If we are to count things together, the theory goes, we must disregard everything that differentiates them and treat them as being exactly similar. But, Frege objects, if we abstract from the characteristics which differentiate things, we are left not with the number of the things distinguished, but with a common concept under which they all fall.

If, for example, in considering a white cat and a black cat, I disregard the properties which serve to distinguish them, then I get presumably the concept 'cat'. Even if I proceed to bring them both under this concept and call them, I suppose, units, the white one still remains white just the same, and the black black. I may not think about their colours, or I may propose to make no inference from their difference in this respect, but for all that the cats do not become colourless and they remain different precisely as before. (FA, p. 45.)

If, in order to be countable units, two things have to be alike in every respect, then there will be no units at all, because no two things are completely alike.

In fact, it is not true that, in order to be countable, units must have all their properties in common. What *is* true is that in order to be counted together, two things have to fall under some single concept (as the two cats fall under the single concept *cat*); and this is something which Frege will exploit when he comes to give his own account of number.[2] But that is quite different from saying that units have to be totally alike.

Frege's train of thought here is not altogether easy to follow, because the German word '*Gleichheit*', which he uses for the

---

2. Frege quotes Spinoza as pointing out that a man who has in his hand a cent and a dollar will not think of the number two unless he can bring both cent and dollar under a single name, 'coin' (FA, p. 62).

property to be ascribed to units, may mean 'identity', 'equality' or 'similarity'. Sometimes his text reads more convincingly if we translate the adjective '*gleich*' as 'identical', sometimes if we translate it as 'alike'. This may make one suspect an equivocation in his argument. But in reality, the ambiguity is not damaging. For Frege accepted Leibniz's principle of the identity of indiscernibles: the principle, that is to say, that no two things have all their properties in common.[3] If this is accepted, it follows that if whatever is true of A is true of B, then A is identical with B. On this principle, total similarity between units would amount to identity. Hence he can sum up his objection thus: 'If we call the things to be numbered units, then the assertion that units are absolutely alike is false. That they are alike in one or other respect is true enough but of no interest.' (FA, p. 58.)

Some philosophers have taken the essential feature of units to be not similarity but diversity. Thus W.S. Jevons is quoted as saying, 'It has often been said that units are units in respect of being perfectly similar to each other; but though they may be perfectly similar in some respects, they must be different in at least one point, otherwise they would be incapable of plurality. If three coins were so similar that they occupied the same place at the same time, they would not be three coins, but one.' (FA, p. 46.)

But the insistence that units must be different encounters as many difficulties as the demand that units must be alike. If 5 is regarded as a set of five units, one might denote it by the symbol '1 + 1 + 1 + 1 + 1'. But the units of which 5 is composed must be regarded as distinct from each other; and so the symbol

---

3. Frege continued to accept this interpretation of equality and identity throughout his life. Thus, in the second volume of *Grundgesetze der Arithmetik* he wrote: 'In regard to the *equals* sign we shall do well to keep to our convention that equality is complete coincidence, identity. Of course bodies equal in volume are not identical, but they have the same volume. The signs on either side of the *equals* sign must thus in this case be taken as signs not for bodies but for their volumes, or for the numerical values obtained by measuring in terms of the same unit volume.'

might be better written, in accordance with a further suggestion of Jevons, as '1′ + 1″ + 1‴ + 1⁗ + 1‴″'. Here the repeated use of '1' is meant to bring out the similarity between the units, and the primes are meant to bring out the difference. Unfortunately, Frege says, the latter undo the work of the former. There is no reason why we should not instead have written '$a + b + c + d + e$'. 'So', says Frege, 'our one slips through our fingers; we are left with the objects in all their particularity.' Nothing has been gained by calling the objects 'units'.

The use of the symbol '1' in Jevons's notation was meant to indicate the number one; but the number one is quite different from a unit or countable thing. There is only one number one; '1' is a proper name which does not admit of a plural any more than does 'Frederick the Great' or 'the element gold'. '1' cannot be regarded as a symbol for different distinct objects, for Iceland, Aldebaran, Solon and so on. To use the same symbol to indicate a unit and to represent the number one, as Jevons does, is to court absurdity.

To explain the way in which, in numerical units, distinguishability is to be combined with similarity, Jevons introduces a notion of numerical abstraction.

It consists in abstracting the character of the difference from which plurality arises, retaining merely the fact. When I speak of *three men* I need not at once specify the marks by which each may be known from each. Those marks must exist if they are really three men and not one and the same, and in speaking of them as many I imply the existence of the requisite differences. Abstract number, then, is the *empty form of difference*. (FA, p. 55; quoting *The Principles of Science*. London, 1874, p. 156.)

Frege observes that if this means that we have first to form a whole and then abstract from the distinguishing properties of its constituents it is difficult to see how we could arrive at a number like 10 000, for it would be beyond our powers to grasp so many differences at once and retain the fact of their existence. What is meant by 'the empty form of difference'? Does a proposition like '*a* is different from *b*' give us a number 2? 'The Earth has two poles' must mean something quite different from 'The North Pole is different from the South', as we see if we reflect that either proposition could be true without the other.

How is numerical abstraction to give us the numbers 0 and 1? If we consider the Moon, then we can perhaps arrive by a process of abstraction at various concepts, for example, satellite of the Earth, heavenly body, body and so on. But by this route we never reach the number 1: it is not a concept the Moon falls under, as it falls under the concepts *satellite* and *body*. Matters are even worse in the case of 0, where there is no object from which to start our process of abstracting. It is no good saying that 0 and 1 are not numbers in the same sense as 2 and 3. Anything which answers the question 'How many?' counts as a number, and 0 is a perfectly good answer to the question 'How many moons has such and such a planet?'

Three theories have now been examined and found wanting: that number is a property of things, that number is a subjective creation, and that number is a set of units. None of these theories provides an answer to the question: When we make a statement of a number, what is it of which we are stating something?

It is at section 46 of the *Foundations* that Frege begins to set out his own answer. He starts from the observations used earlier to refute the idea that number was a property of physical things or phenomena.

While looking at one and the same external phenomenon, I can say with equal truth both 'It is a copse' and 'It is five trees', or both 'Here are four companies' and 'Here are 500 men'. Now what changes here from one judgement to the other is neither any individual item, nor the whole, the agglomeration of them, but only my nomenclature. But that is itself only a sign that one concept has been substituted for another. (FA, p. 59.)

This suggests as an answer to the as yet unresolved question: the content of a statement of number is an assertion about a concept. This comes out most clearly in the case where the number in question is zero.

If I say 'Venus has zero moons', there simply does not exist any moon or agglomeration of moons for anything to be asserted of; but what happens is that a property is assigned to the *concept* 'moon of Venus', namely that of including nothing under it. (FA, p. 59.)

Frege's thesis that an assignment of number is a statement about a concept should not be misunderstood as a version of the thesis that number is something subjective. A Fregean concept is something objective, not a psychological entity like a mental image. Other statements about concepts are possible beside number statements. For instance, a generalization such as 'All whales are mammals' is not a statement about animals, but an assertion of the subordination of the concept of *whale* to that of *mammal*.

However true it may be that our proposition can only be verified by observing particular animals, that proves nothing as to its content; to decide what it is about we do not need to know whether it is true or not, nor for what reasons we believe it to be true. If, then, a concept is something objective, an assertion about a concept can have a factual content. (FA, p. 61.)

Frege goes on to show that a number of the puzzling features revealed in the earlier discussion are easily explained if we accept that a statement of number is an assertion about a concept. Earlier examples made it look as if one thing could have more than one number; but once we realize number belongs to concepts, not things, we find that numbers are mutually exclusive. One concept cannot have two different numbers assigned to it any more than one object can be red and green all over.

It is a misunderstanding to think that numbers are reached by abstraction; the most we can say is that numbers belong to concepts, and concepts can be acquired by abstraction. Hence abstraction does often precede a judgement of number. But abstraction is certainly not the only way of forming concepts:

we can form concepts by combining defining characteristics, and in such a case it may be that nothing falls under the concept. If that were not so, we would never be able to make true denials of existence, such as 'There are no unicorns'.

It seemed odd that number appeared to be predicable of physical objects and mental objects, of the temporal and timeless alike. But that is not really what happens in number-statements. Numbers are assigned not to these varied objects, but to the concepts under which they fall.

When an object falls under a concept, that does not mean that the word for the concept is a name of the thing. Tibbles is a cat, and falls under the concept *cat*; but 'cat' is not his name. Frege will allow that we call him 'the cat'; but, he says, a concept word conjoined with a definite article counts as a proper name and ceases to be a concept word.

A concept does not cease to be a concept simply because only one thing falls under it, which thing, accordingly, is completely determined by it. It is to concepts of just this kind (for example, satellite of the Earth) that the number one belongs, which is a number in the same sense as 2 and 3. With a concept the question is always whether anything, and if so what, falls under it. With a proper name such questions make no sense. (FA, pp. 63-4.)

When Frege says that number is a property of a concept, or more correctly that a statement of number assigns a property to a concept, it is important to bear in mind that he makes a systematic distinction between a property of a concept and a component (*Merkmal*) of a concept. *Right-angled* is a component of the concept *right-angled triangle*, but it is not a property of that concept; it is a property of the triangles that fall under it. But the proposition that there are no equilateral right-angled triangles does state a property of the concept *equilateral right-angled triangle*: it assigns to it the number zero (nought).

In a passage of great philosophical importance (FA, p. 65) Frege propounds an analogy between existence and number. 'Affirmation of existence', he says, 'is in fact nothing but denial of the number nought.' What he means is that an affirmation of existence (for example, 'Angels exist' or 'There are [such things as] angels') is an assertion that a concept (for example *Angel*) has something falling under it. And to say that a concept has something falling under it is to say that the number which belongs to that concept is something other than zero.

It is because existence is a property of concepts, Frege says, that the ontological argument for the existence of God breaks down. That is to say, that-there-is-a-God cannot be a component of the concept *God*, nor can it be a component of that concept that-there-is-only-one-God. But if in fact there is one and only one God, that is a property, in Frege's terminology, of the concept *God*.

Though the ontological argument fails, the reason for its failure is not that it is never possible to make an inference from the components of a concept to its properties. Frege himself has just inferred from the components of the concept *equilateral right-angled triangle* that it has the property of possessing the number zero. Perhaps there may also be cases where one can infer from the component characteristics of a concept to existence or to uniqueness. What is true is that this can never be as direct a matter as assigning a component characteristic of a concept as a property to an object falling under it (for example, deciding that a figure which falls under the concept *right-angled triangle* is triangular).

Moreover, there can be concepts of which existence and singularity are themselves components. But these would be concepts of a special kind: Frege introduces the name 'second-order concept' for them. Suppose we collected under a single concept all concepts under which there falls only one object; in that case, oneness, in the sense of uniqueness, would be a component of this new concept. Under it would fall the concept *moon of the earth*, though not the Moon itself. 'In this way', Frege says, 'we can make one concept fall under another higher or, so to say, second-order concept.' This relation is quite different from the subordination of species to genus (for example the relationship of the concept *moon* to the concept *satellite*).

We can offer a sense to 'unit' which will account for the apparently irreconcilable properties which were needed if numbers were to be defined in terms of units. Why not say that a concept is the unit relative to the number which belongs to it?[4]

We can now give a definitive answer to the question whether units are indiscernible or distinguishable. In the proposition 'Jupiter has four moons' the units are identical, in the sense that the unit is the single concept *moon of Jupiter*. Under this concept fall the four moons, I, II, III, IV. The unit to which I relates is identical to the unit to which II relates, and so on. But when we say that the units are distinguishable, what we mean is that each of the moons, each of the things numbered, is distinguishable from each other. So we can do justice to each of the apparently irreconcilable demands, that units should be identical, and that they should be distinguishable.

---

4. Not every concept will present a unit: the concept *dog* does, because 'count the dogs' makes sense; but the concept *red* does not, because 'count the reds' sets no determinate task. 'Only a concept which isolates what falls under it in a definite manner, and which does not permit any arbitrary division of it into parts, can be a unit relative to a finite number.' (FA, p. 66.)

CHAPTER 5

THE FOUNDATIONS OF ARITHMETIC, II

With the fourth chapter of *The Foundations of Arithmetic* there is an abrupt change of pace. Hitherto, though no words have been wasted, Frege has dealt in a leisurely fashion with mistaken views of the status of arithmetic and has allowed his own thesis about the nature of number to emerge implicitly as a result of his detailed criticism of others. His arguments, though often impatient and sometimes sarcastic, almost always strike the reader as fair and convincing.

Now all this changes. The speed of discussion accelerates violently; Frege begins to develop his own theories with astonishing rapidity. Bizarre questions are raised with the minimum of preparation; counter-intuitive theses are defended by the barest skeleton of argument.

Section 55, in particular, gives the impression of a breakneck rush towards a conclusion. The general concept of number has now been defined, or, rather, we have learned that the content of a statement of number is an assertion about a concept. The task that remains is to define the individual numbers 0 and 1, and the notion of increase by one. For it has been agreed that from these elements all the numbers can be derived. Frege instantly presents us with three definitions which appear to meet these requirements.

(a) The number 0. The number 0 belongs to a concept F if no matter what a may be, a does not fall under F.

(b) The number 1. The number 1 belongs to a concept F if it is not the case that whatever a may be, a does not fall under F;

but it is the case that if *a* falls under *F* and *b* falls under *F*, then *a* is the same as *b*.

(c) The definition of *n* + 1 in terms of *n*. The number *n* + 1 belongs to a concept *F* if there is an object *a* which falls under *F*, such that the number *n* belongs to the concept 'falling under *F*, but not being the same as *a*'.

Having read, and digested, these definitions, we almost expect Frege to bring the book to an end, his task completed at this point. But two things bring the reader up short.

First, there is the subheading given to this first section of the chapter: 'Every individual number is a self-subsistent object.' We wonder how this is to be reconciled with the conclusion of the book hitherto, that is, the content of a statement of number is an assertion about a concept. Frege has made a consistent and systematic distinction between concept and object. How can a number be an object if a statement of number is an assertion about a concept? Clearly, some detailed explanation must be forthcoming if these two statements are to be reconciled.

Secondly, Frege himself at once goes on to make clear that the definitions offered do not solve the problem of number. But our puzzlement is increased, rather than diminished, by his reasoning.

Strictly speaking we do not know the sense of the expression 'the number *n* belongs to the concept *G*' any more than we do that of the expression 'the number (*n* + 1) belongs to the concept *F*'. We can, of course, by using the last two definitions together, say what is meant by
  'the number 1 + 1 belongs to the concept *F*'
and then, using this, give the sense of the expression
  'the number 1 + 1 + 1 belongs to the concept *F*'
and so on; but we can never – to take a crude example – decide by means of our definitions whether any concept has the number Julius Caesar belonging to it, or whether that same familiar conqueror of Gaul is a number or is not. (FA, p. 68.)

A common reaction on first reading this is to wonder whether it matters that the proffered definition does not settle the question about Julius Caesar. Surely, it is no small thing to have found a definition which will catch all the natural numbers; if it catches a few other things as well, no great harm is done. And since we know for certain that Julius Caesar is not a number, we can surely risk a bet that a definition which so well fits genuine numbers will not turn out to apply to him as well.

Such insouciance would be misplaced. To see this, consider a different kind of definition which *would* have allowed us to settle the question whether Julius Caesar is a number. We are all familiar with definitions of the form 'A human is a rational animal'; definitions which, in Frege's terms, set out the components of a concept. Someone might offer a definition of number in the same style. It might perhaps begin 'a number is an immaterial object which . . .'. Whatever might be said for or against such a definition, it is clear that it would rule out Julius Caesar as a number. For Julius Caesar, as a human being, is an animal; and no animal is an immaterial object.

Now it would be regarded as a serious objection to a definition of this kind if it turned out to apply to things which did not fall under the concept to be defined. It was long ago observed that 'featherless biped' was an inadequate definition of 'human', since on that definition a plucked chicken would turn out to be a human being. It is, therefore, a genuine defect in a definition of number if it leaves open the possibility of Julius Caesar being a number, even though we may know intuitively that that is not a possibility but an absurdity.

The position is this. The suggested definition gives us a procedure for arriving at each member of the series of natural numbers. We know, from what we have learned from Leibniz, that every natural number is accessible by this procedure. What we do *not* know is that *only* natural numbers are accessible by this procedure. It is this gap in our knowledge that the invocation of Julius Caesar is intended to dramatize.

Moreover, though we know that for any number n we will be able to find a concept F such that n belongs to it, we cannot yet show that n is the only number that belongs to F. 'We cannot',

Frege says, 'by the aid of our suggested definitions prove that, if the number *a* belongs to the concept *F* and the number *b* belongs to the same concept, then necessarily *a = b*.' Once more, the notion that two different numbers might belong to the same concept is so obviously absurd that we might be tempted not to worry that our definition has not ruled it out. But once again, the insouciance would be misplaced. What we are trying to capture in our definitions is our intuitive notion of number, which includes precisely this knowledge that a concept can have only one number at a time.

A great deal of arithmetic remains uncaptured by our definitions. Until we have proved that only one number can belong to each concept, we cannot justify the expression '*The* number belonging to the concept *F*' and therefore we would find it impossible to prove any numerical identities. Frege concludes:

It is only an illusion that we have defined 0 and 1; in reality we have only fixed the sense of the phrases
    'the number 0 belongs to'
    'the number 1 belongs to'
but we have no authority to pick out the 0 and 1 here as self-subsistent objects that can be recognized as the same again. (FA, p. 68.)

Frege now goes on to explain what he means by calling a number a 'self-subsistent object', and how this can be reconciled with the statement that the content of a statement of number is an assertion about a concept.

In the proposition 'the number 0 belongs to the concept *F*', 0 is only an element in the predicate (taking the concept *F* to be the real subject). For this reason I have avoided calling a number such as 0 or 1 or 2 a *property* of a concept. (FA, p. 68.)

For Frege, then, a number is not a property of a thing, and it is not a property of a concept. A number *n belongs to* a concept, on this theory, but the property of the concept is not the number *n* itself, but rather the property of *having the number n belonging to it*. Existence and uniqueness, we have already been told (FA, p. 65), are properties of concepts. These two properties are, for instance, properties of the concept *moon of the Earth*. The terminology is a little uncomfortable: what Frege really should say is that to assert the existence of an object, or the uniqueness of an object, is to make an assertion not about an object but about a concept. What he means, however, is in this context quite clear: a concept has the property of existence if it has at least one object falling under it (that is, if the number 0 does not belong to it); a concept has the property of uniqueness if, in addition to having the property of existence, it has at most one object falling under it (that is, if the number 1 belongs to it). But the properties of the concept are not the numbers 1 and 0, but the having of the number 1, and the not having of the number 0.

A number, then, is not a property; but what is meant by saying that it is a self-subsistent object? Frege is first of all at pains to make clear what he does *not* mean. First, it does not mean that numbers are spatial objects, like the Earth and the Moon. But, as Frege has often insisted, a thing does not have to be spatial in order to be objective. 'It is a fact that the number 4 is exactly the same for everyone who deals with it; but that has nothing to do with being spatial. Not every objective object has a place.' (FA, p. 72.) Secondly, it does not mean that we can have a mental image of a number. If we think of a green field, and then replace 'a' with 'one', nothing is added to our image. If we imagine the printed word 'gold' no number may come to mind; if we are asked how many letters it contains, the number 4 presents itself as the answer, but nothing changes in the image. The point is clearest with the number zero. We cannot form an image of no stars; the image of an overcast sky is not such an image.

It is of course true that images of all kinds do crowd into our minds when we are doing arithmetic or calculating numbers. We may have images of dots on a dice, or of measuring rods reaching between the Earth and the Sun. But these images will not help us in the least to grasp the nature of small numbers, or the distance between the Earth and the Sun. Even so concrete a thing as the Earth cannot have an image formed of it which is more than a mere symbol.

Time and again we are led by our thought beyond the scope of our imagination, without thereby forfeiting the support we need for our inferences. Even if, as seems to be the case, it is impossible for men such as we are to think without images, it is still possible for their connexion with what we are thinking of to be entirely superficial, arbitrary and conventional. (FA, p. 71.)

In the introduction to the *Foundations* Frege had announced three fundamental principles to guide his enquiry: to separate logic and psychology; never to ask for the meaning of a word in isolation, but only in the context of a proposition; and never to confuse concept and object. All three principles are brought to bear in the argument that numbers are self-subsistent objects.

The question at issue manifestly gets its whole point from the distinction between concept and object. Our reluctance to accept that numbers are objects and not concepts arises, Frege believes, from our inclination to ask for the meaning of words in isolation. This inclination leads us to look for an image to be the meaning of a word, and that in its turn is one of the ways in which we confuse logic with psychology. If we can find no image evoked by an isolated word, or only irrelevant ones, then we are apt to deny that any object corresponds to the word in reality.

But we ought always to keep before our eyes a complete proposition. Only in a proposition have the words really a meaning. It may be that mental pictures float before us for a while, but these need not correspond to the logical elements in the judgement. It is enough if the proposition taken as a whole has a sense; it is this that confers on its parts also their content. (FA, p. 71.)

In order to show, then, that a number is a self-subsistent object, Frege must show that numerals, in propositions, behave like proper names. In ordinary speech, numerals often appear as adjectives, as in 'Jupiter has four moons'. But any such sentence can always be rephrased, as in 'The number of Jupiter's moons is four'. Frege has shown, in his analysis of a proposition like 'The number 1 belongs to the concept *moon of the Earth*', that a numeral does not behave like a concept-word. But is that sufficient to show that it is an object-word, a name?

We speak of 'the number one', and Frege claims that the definite article indicates that we are talking of an object. He goes on to say that an individual number shows itself to be a self-subsistent object because 'it forms only a part of what is asserted' (FA, p. 68). But this is not convincing: one might as well say that *belonging* is an object because 'belongs' is only a part of what is asserted of the concept in assignments of number. What Frege really means is that a number is capable of forming the subject of a singular judgement-content (FA, note p. 77). This is, on the face of it, true: we have statements such as '7 is a prime number'. But given that Frege often maintains that ordinary grammar is misleading (as in 'Jupiter has 4 moons') the thesis that numbers are objects needs more support than these facts of everyday idiom.

The crucial feature of an object, for Frege, is that it is something which possesses an identity which is capable of being recognized over and over again. Hence, the most important argument for numbers being objects is that they can be the subject of equations, as $1 + 1 = 2$. Frege takes an equation as a statement of identity: the expressions that flank the equals sign are to be taken as two names of the same object. An equation sign in arithmetic is to be taken as equivalent to the 'is' of identity in ordinary language, as in 'Paris is the capital of France'. In 'the number of Jupiter's moons is four', too, the 'is' should be taken as the 'is' of identity, equivalent to the '$=$' sign. Equations, or identities, are, of all forms of proposition, the ones most typical of arithmetic. It is above all the fact that numbers figure in equations which, for Frege, shows that they are self-subsistent objects (FA, p. 69).

If numbers are self-subsistent objects, and can figure in equations, then there must be propositions which express our recognition of a number as being the same number again. For, quite generally, if we are to use the symbol *a* to signify an object, we must have a criterion for deciding in all cases whether *b* is the same as *a*, even if it is not always in our power to apply this criterion. We must, that is to say, have a criterion of identity for an object of any given kind. In order to establish a criterion of identity for numbers, we have to define the sense of the proposition

The number which belongs to the concept *F* is the same as the number which belongs to the concept *G*.

We must reproduce the content of this proposition without using the expression 'The number which belongs to the concept *F*', for that expression, with its definite article, assumes we have already performed the task of re-identifying a number. Only the successful performance of such a task would entitle us to use the definite article and assign a proper name.

How will we do this? Frege adopts a suggestion made by Hume. 'When two numbers are so combined as that the one has always an unit answering to every unit of the other, we pronounce them equal' (*A Treatise of Human Nature*, I, iii, i). We should define numerical equality (which Frege treats as being the same as numerical identity) in terms of one–one correlation. The number belonging to the concept *F* is the same as the number belonging to *G* if all the items falling under *F* can be correlated one-to-one with all the items falling under *G*. For instance, the number of knives on the table is the same as the number of plates on the table if there is a knife to the right of each plate.

Frege proposes, on the basis of this simple idea, to give a definition of the individual numbers which will avoid the objections made to the earlier proposals made by other philosophers. He proposes to define the concept of number in terms of the concept of numerical identity. This may seem a perverse proceeding. It seems natural to think that we understand what 'the same *F*' means by understanding what '*F*' means, and by understanding what 'the same' means; thus, we understand what 'the same book' means by having a concept of *book* and by possessing the general concept of identity. There is surely a general concept of identity, since the concept applies to many other things besides numbers. Should we not expect to understand 'the same number' by applying our general concept of identity to the concept of number?

Frege replies that we do not yet have a concept of number. What he is proposing to do is to define 'number' in terms of a definition of '. . . is the same number as . . .'. To show that this is not an inappropriate method of proceeding, he invites us to consider a different concept, that of the direction of a line.

Two lines are parallel to each other if they have the same direction. Now, should we define parallelism in terms of direction, or should direction be defined in terms of parallelism? The argument presented above would suggest that the appropriate starting point would be the concept of *direction*: once we know what direction is, it will be easy to settle whether two lines have the same direction.

However, do we have a concept of direction? Since it is a geometrical concept, it is presumably to be given in intuition. But, Frege asks, do we have an intuition of the direction of a straight line? 'Of a straight line, certainly; but do we distinguish in our intuition between this straight line and something else, its direction?' On the other hand, there is no difficulty in summoning up an image of two parallel straight lines.

Instead, therefore, of defining parallelism in terms of identity of direction, we should perhaps move in the opposite direction, and say that 'the direction of line *a* is identical with the direction of line *b*' is to mean the same as 'line *a* is parallel to line *b*'. But if we do this, how can we be sure that our definition of identity of direction will not fall foul of the concept of identity itself? This concept is expressed in well-known laws which, Frege says, are well summed up in the famous dictum of Leibniz:

Things are the same as each other, of which one can be substituted for the other without loss of truth.[1]

---

1. It is remarkable that Frege does not point out the confusion of sign

We can defend, therefore, our definition of 'direction' if we can show that it is possible, if line *a* is parallel to line *b*, to substitute everywhere 'the direction of *b*' for 'the direction of *a*' without loss of truth.

There remains, however, a serious difficulty. Our definition enables us to recognize the direction of *a* as an object, and to recognize this as the same object again if it turns up in another guise as the direction of *b*. But our definition does not enable us to decide, for instance, whether England is the same as the direction of the Earth's axis. The difficulty is analogous to the problem of deciding whether or not Julius Caesar was a number. 'Naturally', Frege says, 'no one is going to confuse England with the direction of the Earth's axis; but this is no thanks to our definition of direction.'

We still lack a concept of direction here, as in the earlier case we lacked a concept of number. If we had such a concept, we could lay down that the proposition

The direction of *a* is identical with *q*

should be denied if *q* was not a direction, while if it is a direction it is to be affirmed or denied in accordance with our previous definition. But we are not yet in a position to give, without circularity, a definition of what it is to be a direction.

To resolve these difficulties, Frege now makes a proposal of considerable philosophical significance. He observes that if line *a* is parallel to line *b*, then the extension of the concept 'line parallel to line *a*' is identical with the extension of the concept 'line parallel to line *b*', and conversely, if the extensions of these two concepts are identical, then *a* is parallel to *b*. He therefore proposes to define the direction of line *a* as: the extension of the concept *parallel to line a*.

To evaluate this, we must first clarify what is meant by the

-----

and thing signified here. Instead, he makes a number of remarks which are necessary only because the German word '*gleich*' means both 'like' and 'identical'.

extension of a concept. Frege says, 'I assume that it is known what the extension of a concept is.' For logicians prior to Frege, a concept's extension is the totality of objects which fall under it: thus, the extension of the concept *cat* is the set of all cats, and the extension of the concept *moon of Jupiter* is the set of Jupiter's moons.[2]

Thus, when Frege says that the direction of line *a* is the extension of the concept *parallel to line a* he is defining the direction of the line as the class of all lines parallel to it. We need not concern ourselves with the merits of this definition: in Frege's text it is merely to prepare the way for a definition of number which is likewise to be in terms of the extension of concepts.

The notion of the extension of a concept seems clear enough where the concept in question is one corresponding to a simple, one-place predicate, such as '. . . is a cat'. But since the *Concept Script* Frege had introduced the notion of two-place predicates, such as '. . . is to the right of '. . .' or '. . .' is heavier than '. . .'. To these two-place predicates there correspond relational concepts, and it is these concepts which are about to play a crucial role in Frege's definition of number. But the notion of the extension of a relational concept demands further explanation.

Frege points out that the propositions

> The Earth is more massive than the Moon,
> The Sun is more massive than the Earth,

both express judgements which contain the relation-concept *more massive than*. In each judgement a pair of objects is correlated with each other by means of this relation.

2. If nothing falls under a concept, does that mean that the concept has no extension? Not necessarily. Shortly before Frege, Jevons had introduced the notion of the null (or empty) class, a class with no members. Frege develops this idea in his own work, as we shall see.

Each individual pair of correlated objects stands to the relation-concept much as an individual object stands to the concept under which it falls – we might call them the subject of the relation-concept. Only here the subject is a composite one. (FA, p. 82.)

That is, we are to think of the pairs (Earth, Moon), (Sun, Earth) and so on as falling under the relation-concept *more massive than* in the way in which the individuals Tibbles, Smudge etc. fall under the concept *cat*. The extension, therefore, of this relation-concept will be the set of ordered pairs of objects between which the relation holds.

We are now prepared for Frege's introduction of a definition of number analogous to his definition of direction.

The number which belongs to the concept F is the extension of the concept 'equivalent to the concept F'. (FA, p. 79.)

Frege explains that what he means by saying that two concepts F and G are equivalent is that the objects which fall under F can be correlated one-to-one with the objects which fall under G – in the way that, when a table has been well laid with a knife beside every plate, objects falling under the concept *knife* can be correlated one-to-one with objects falling under the concept *plate*.

Before evaluating Frege's definition, let us illustrate its import in a simple case. The number which belongs to the concept *evangelist* is 4: there were four evangelists, Matthew, Mark, Luke and John. There are many concepts which are, in Frege's sense, equivalent to the concept *evangelist*: for instance, *point of the compass, suit at bridge, fundamental force*. By Frege's definition then, the number which belongs to the concept *evangelist* is the extension of the concept *equivalent to the concept evangelist*. Since only a concept can be equivalent to a concept, this extension will be a class of concepts: the class of concepts which, like those listed above, apply to four and only four objects. Frege's definition will have the upshot that the number four is the class of all concepts which have – in this sense – the property of fourness. It will be both a class of concepts (the ones with the property of fourness) and the extension of a higher-order concept (the concept of fourness itself).

At first sight this definition seems both incongruous and circular. But the circularity is only apparent, and the appropriateness of the definition is best shown by deriving from it the well-known properties of numbers. Above, we used, to illustrate the import of Frege's definition, the number four; but in the definition itself, and in the crucial notion of the equality between concepts, no number is smuggled in. As Frege says, if a waiter wishes to be certain of laying exactly as many knives as plates, he has no need to count either; all he needs to do is to take care that there is just one knife beside each plate. Awareness of the one–one correlation can be prior to, and need not presuppose, awareness of the number of the correlated objects. Hence number can be defined, without circularity, in terms of one–one correlation.

One–one correlation is now formally defined in two stages. First there is the definition of correlation:

If every object which falls under the concept F stands in the relation Φ to an object falling under the concept G and if to every object which falls under G there stands in the relation Φ an object falling under F, then the objects falling under F and under G are correlated with each other by the relation Φ. (FA, p. 83.)

For instance, if every husband is married to some wife, and every wife is married to some husband, then husbands and wives are correlated by marriage.

This definition gives us correlation, not one–one correlation. The proposition just enunciated is just as true in a polygamous or polyandrous society as it is in a monogamous one; and of course it is only in a monogamous society that husbands and wives are correlated one-to-one, so that the number of husbands is the same as the number of wives.

To go from correlation to one–one correlation, we have to add two further propositions.

> If *d* stands in the relation Φ to *a*, and if *d* stands in the
> relation Φ to *e*, then whatever *d, a* and *e* may be *a* = *e*.
> If *d* stands in the relation Φ to *a*, and if *b* stands in the
> relation Φ to *a*, then whatever *d, b*, and *a* may be *d* = *b*.

We have thus defined one–one correlation in purely logical
terms, without using any concepts drawn from arithmetic. With
the definition that a concept *F* is equivalent to a concept *G* if
there is a relation which correlates, one-to-one, the objects
falling under *F* with the objects falling under *G*, we have all
that is necessary for the following definition:

> The number which belongs to the concept *F* is the extension
> of the concept *equivalent to the concept F*.

There is therefore nothing circular in the definition of number
which Frege now triumphantly offers:

> *n* is a number

is to mean the same as the expression

> there exists a concept such that *n* is the number which
> belongs to it.

Before going on to define the individual numbers it only
remains for Frege to show that the number which belongs to the
concept *F* is identical with the number which belongs to the
concept *G* if the concept *F* is equivalent to the concept *G*. This
sounds like a tautology, but in fact needs a proof; but the proof,
though a little complicated, is quite unproblematic (FA, section
73).

Having given a general definition of a number as a set of
equivalent concepts, Frege can go on to define the individual
numbers by finding a suitable concept to specify each set. As we
have seen above, the number four could, on Frege's model, be
defined as the set of concepts equivalent to the concept *evangelist*. Indeed, any of the other concepts under which four objects
fall will do equally well: since if any two concepts are equivalent
to a third they are equivalent to each other. (Given Frege's

special definition of 'equivalent', this is not a tautology, but needs proving; however, its proof presents no difficulty (FA, pp. 85–6). But a concept such as *evangelist* would be useless for Frege's purpose of reducing arithmetic to logic; because it is no part of logic that there were four and only four gospel-makers. Moreover, there is no guarantee that we will be able to find an empirical concept to match each of the endless series of natural numbers.

What Frege does is to carry out the Leibnizian programme of defining all the natural numbers in terms of 0, 1 and increase by one. He begins by defining zero. He could have defined it as, say, the set of concepts equal to the concept *unicorn*. For since there are no unicorns, the class of unicorns has zero members. But once again he is looking for a definition which will involve only terms taken from logic. He defines zero as follows:

0 is the number which belongs to the concept 'not identical with itself'. (FA, p. 87.)

Since each thing is identical with itself, nothing falls under the concept *not identical with itself*. Since this is an analytic truth which we know a priori, Frege can make use of it to give a purely logical definition of zero.

Two objections present themselves to his definition. First, if we say 'no objects are non-self-identical', is not 'no' simply a synonym for zero, and so is not the definition circular? (cf. FA, pp. 67). Secondly, is not the notion of non-self-identity self-contradictory and therefore absurd?

Both objections are easily answered. First, we can rewrite our proposition thus

Whatever *x* may be, it is not the case that *x* is not identical with *x*.

In this reformulation, there is nothing which looks like a synonym for '0'. Secondly, there is nothing wrong in using self-contradictory concepts, as long as we do not deceive ourselves into thinking that something falls under them.

All that logic can demand for rigour of proof is that the limits of application of a concept should be sharp, so that it is determined with respect to each object whether it falls under it or not. But this demand is satisfied by concepts which, like 'not identical with itself', contain a contradiction, for of every object we know that it does not fall under any such concept. (FA, p. 87.)

By Frege's definition of number in general, if 0 is the number which belongs to the concept *non-self-identical*, it is the set of concepts equivalent to that concept. We need to show that every concept under which no object falls is equivalent to every other concept under which no object falls. But how can this be done, since equivalence was defined in terms of the one–one correlation of objects falling under concepts?

Let us look more closely at the definition of correlation. It can be set out as follows.

There is a relation Φ such that:

(1) Whatever x may be, if x falls under F then it stands in the relation Φ to some G.

(2) Whatever y may be, if y falls under G then it stands in the relation Φ to some F.

Here, Frege explains, the 'if' is to be understood in the truth-functional way which was introduced in the *Begriffschrift*; that is, 'If p then q' is to be taken as true provided only that it is not the case that p is true and q is false. Since, in the case in point, whatever x may be it does not fall under F, and whatever y may be it does not fall under G, both (1) and (2) in the definition of correlation will come out true, and they will do so no matter what relation we put in the place of the variable Φ. The propositions which need to be added to make correlation into a one–one correlation will likewise turn out true in the same vacuous manner. Hence, if no object falls under F and no object falls under G, then the concepts F and G will be equivalent. It is also not difficult to show that any concept under which some object falls is not equivalent to any concept under which no object falls. Accordingly the definition of zero can be allowed to stand.

To get from zero to one, Frege must next define the relation holding between adjacent members of the number series. He defines '*n* is an immediate successor of *m*' thus:

there exists a concept *F*, and an object falling under it *x*, such that the number which belongs to the concept *F* is *n* and the number which belongs to the concept 'falling under *F* but not identical with *x*' is *m*. (FA, p. 89.)

The import of this can be brought out by using, once again, a non-logical example. Take the concept *Tudor monarch*. The number belonging to this concept, we know from English history, is 5. There are, that is to say, five objects which fall under it. Let us take one such object: King Henry VIII. The number which belongs to the concept *Tudor monarch not identical with Henry VIII* is 4. And 5 is indeed the immediate successor of 4 in the number series. Once again, our example of the concept *F* is useless for Frege's purposes, since it is drawn from history and not logic.

Instead, Frege takes the concept *identical with zero*. There is one and only one object which falls under this concept, namely zero. Now what is the number of things which fall under the concept, but are not identical with zero? What, that is to say, is the number which belongs to the concept *identical with zero but not identical with zero*? Obviously, the number is zero.

If we now define 1 as the number which belongs to the concept *identical with zero* we have the following.

There is a concept, *identical with zero*, and an object falling under it, zero, such that the number which belongs to the concept *identical with zero* is 1, and the number which belongs to the concept *identical with zero but not identical with zero* is 0.

By the definition of 'successor' this means that 1 immediately succeeds 0 in the number series. (A few extra steps are necessary to show that *only* 1 immediately succeeds 0, so that we can speak of 1 as *the* successor of 0.)

In effect, Frege defines the numbers in the following way:

0 is the number belonging to the concept *non-self-identical*,
1 is the number belonging to the concept *identical with zero*,
2 is the number belonging to the concept *identical with 0 or 1*,
3 is the number belonging to the concept *identical with 0, 1 or 2*.

To show that this pattern can be repeated to generate the endless number series, he has to prove that after every number in the series of natural numbers there follows another number, and thus that the number series is infinite. For this purpose he draws upon the definition of the ancestral relation he had given in the *Concept Script*.

Given a relation Φ we can define another relation expressible as

$$y \text{ follows in the } \Phi\text{-series after } x$$

or

$$x \text{ comes in the } \Phi\text{-series before } y.$$

We can, for example, define the notions of *descendant* and *ancestor* in terms of the relation of *parent*.

Frege's procedure for providing such a definition goes as follows. First, he defines the notion of hereditary property: a property is hereditary in the Φ-series when, for any d, if the property belongs to d, then it belongs to whatever d stands in the relation Φ to. Humanity, for instance, is hereditary in the series parent–child: any child of a human is itself a human. Secondly, Frege says that y follows in the Φ-series after x, provided that y has every Φ-hereditary property that x has. If again we take the relation Φ as the relation of parent to child, we can say that Adam's descendants are all those who have all the hereditary properties that every child of Adam has.

In order to make use of the ancestral relation in generating the number series, we have to take the relation Φ to be the relation, already defined, which one number stands in to another when it immediately succeeds it. In this case, the Φ-series will be the series of natural numbers. We can then say that 'y follows in the series of natural numbers after x' is to mean the same as 'y has all those properties which belong to any immediate successor of x and which are hereditary in the series of natural numbers'. The immediate successor of a number will be, as it were, the child of that number; the other numbers succeeding it in the series of natural numbers will be, as it were, its descendants.

Frege now introduces the concept of *being a member of the series of natural numbers ending with n*; a falls under this concept if n is either identical with a or follows it in the series of natural numbers. It can be proved – and Frege gives a sketch of the proof – that the number which belongs to that concept immediately follows n in the series of natural numbers. For any n, then, there will be a number immediately following it in the series, and therefore there is no end to the series.

The procedure which Frege follows is now customarily known by the name 'mathematical induction'. Mathematical induction involves an induction base and an induction step. In Frege's system, the induction base is provided by the number zero. It has already been shown that the number of the series of natural numbers ending with zero follows in the series of natural numbers immediately after zero; for one is the number belonging to the series of natural numbers ending in zero.

The induction step is as follows.

If a is the immediate successor of d, and if it is true that the number belonging to the concept *member of the series of natural numbers ending with d* is the immediate successor of d, then it is also true of a that the number belonging to the concept *member of the series of natural numbers ending with a* is the immediate successor of a.

It is this step which enables us to move, without interruption, in the series of natural numbers beginning with zero, from each n to $n + 1$. But we still need to prove that no object which is a member of the series of natural numbers beginning with zero can follow in the series of natural numbers after itself. It can be shown from the definitions, though Frege does not do so, that this is the case.

Frege now defines 'n is a finite number' as equivalent to 'n is a member of the series of natural numbers beginning with 0'. With this definition, he can conclude that no finite number follows in the series of natural numbers after itself.

This, in turn, allows him to define infinite numbers. The number which belongs to the concept *finite number* is, as Georg Cantor had shown, an infinite number: it is commonly symbolized by aleph-zero, $\aleph_0$. According to Frege's definition, to say that the number which belongs to the concept F is aleph-zero means that there exists a relation which correlates one-to-one the objects falling under the concept F with the finite numbers. This has a clear sense, and that is enough to justify the use of the symbol aleph-zero and to assure it of a meaning. Aleph-zero is therefore a number which follows in the series of natural numbers after itself.

In the conclusion to the *Foundations*, Frege claims that he has now made it probable that the laws of arithmetic are not only a priori but also analytic. Arithmetic becomes an extension of logic, and every theorem of arithmetic becomes a law of logic. Arithmetic is not one of the physical sciences; laws of number are not laws of nature. In the physical world of nature there are no concepts, no properties of concepts, no numbers. The laws of arithmetic can be called laws of laws of nature; for they assert connections between judgements, and some judgements are laws of nature.

Kant underestimated the fertility of analytic judgements, Frege tells us, because he restricted his consideration to universal affirmative judgements, and he thought of the kind of analysis involved as being the simple resolution of a concept into its characteristic components. But definition in terms of components, Frege says, is the least fruitful form of definition; it defines the boundary of a concept (such as 'human') in terms of other existing concepts (such as 'rational' and 'animal'). The different kinds of definition which have been offered by Frege in the *Foundations* draw boundary lines where none were previously given at all. Hence our knowledge can be genuinely extended by analytic propositions. The truths we prove are contained in the definitions, not like exposed beams in a house, but like plants in their seeds.

We may be surprised that Frege claims nothing more than probability for the thesis that arithmetic is derived from logic. Surely a proof such as he offers, if successful, must provide certainty; and if it does not, it must fail altogether of its purpose. But Frege is not simply being inappropriately modest: he is drawing attention to the informal nature of the proofs in the *Foundations*, which may turn out on closer examination to appeal tacitly to some non-logical premiss at some point in the argument. Frege's proofs are no more logically watertight than the proofs offered by the mathematicians of his day.

[T]he mathematician rests content if every transition to a fresh judgement is self-evidently correct, without enquiring into the nature of this self-evidence, whether it is logical or intuitive. A single such step is often really a whole compendium, equivalent to several simple inferences, and into it there can still creep along with these some elements from intuition. In proofs as we know them, progress is by jumps. (FA, p. 102.)

In order to avoid such jumps, Frege's proofs would have to be given in the symbolism of his *Concept Script*, which is a calculus designed to be operated by a small number of standard moves, so as to prevent any premise creeping into a proof without being noticed. But rigorous proofs of this kind are likely to be found tedious by the general reader to whom the *Foundations* are directed.

At the end of the book, Frege turns very briefly to consider numbers other than natural numbers: negative, fractional, irrational and complex numbers. Most of his attention is devoted to criticizing what he calls the 'formalist' account of these numbers. The target of his criticism is the assumption that a concept is treated as free of contradiction provided that no contradiction has revealed itself. Freedom from contradiction in a concept, in any case, is no guarantee that an object falls under it. The truth is the converse: the only way to prove that a concept is free of contradiction is to produce something that falls under it. It is quite wrong, Frege maintains, to think that the mathematician can simply lay down postulates and assume that they are satisfied. A mathematician is not a god who can create things at will; rather he is like a geographer who can only discover what is there and give it a name.

The formalist's mistake is to confuse concepts and objects.

Nothing prevents us from using the concept 'square root of −1'; but we are not entitled to put the definite article in front of it without more ado and take the expression 'the square root of −1' as having sense. (FA, p. 108.)

What we have to do with complex and irrational numbers is what we did with the natural numbers.

[E]verything will in the end come down to the search for a judgement-content which can be transformed into an equation between the two numbers. In other words, what we must do is to fix the sense of a recognition-judgement for the case of these numbers. (FA, p. 114.)

If we do this then the new numbers, like the natural numbers, will be given to us as the extensions of concepts, and they will be no more mysterious than the positive integers.

Frege concludes his work by saying that his account of numbers accounts for the particular charm of mathematics. It illustrates the sense in which the proper study of reason is reason itself. Nothing is more objective that the laws of arithmetic, and yet:

In arithmetic we are not concerned with objects which we come to know as something alien from without through the medium of the senses, but with objects given directly to our reason and, as its nearest kin, utterly transparent to it. (FA, p. 115.)

CHAPTER 6

FUNCTION, CONCEPT AND OBJECT

The Foundations of Arithmetic was published in 1884. After 1884 Frege published almost nothing for the rest of the decade, except a lecture, 'On Formal Theories of Arithmetic' (CP, p. 112–21). This lecture is mainly devoted to developing the criticisms of formalism which occur in the concluding sections of the *Foundations*.

Two different types of theory, Frege says, may be called 'formal': one is good and the other is bad. The good kind of formal theory of arithmetic is Frege's own theory that arithmetic is derivable from logic. The bad kind of formal theory is one which maintains that signs for numbers like '½' or 'π' are merely empty signs.

No one, Frege says, could really put the formalist theory into practice. Merely calling the numerals 'signs' already suggests that they do signify something. A resolute formalist should call them 'shapes'. If we took seriously the contention that '½' does not designate anything, then it is merely a splash of printer's ink or a splurge of chalk, with various physical and chemical properties. How can it possibly have the property that if added to itself it yields 1? Shall we say that it is given this property by definition? A definition serves to connect a sense with a word: but this sign was supposed to be empty, and therefore to lack content. It is true that it is up to us to give a signification to a sign, and therefore it in part depends on human will what properties the content of a sign has. But these properties are properties of the content, not of the sign itself, and hence, according to the formalist, they will not be properties of the number. What we cannot do is to give things properties by definition.

Someone could just as easily hit upon the idea of branding his fellow-citizen a liar by the simple expedient of a definition. It would then be very easy to prove the truth of his charge. He would merely have to say, 'That follows immediately from my definition.' Indeed: it would follow from the definition just as rigorously as it follows from the definition 'this chalk-figure has the property of yielding 1 when added to itself' that when added to itself, the figure yields 1. (CP, p. 116.)

No definition, Frege was later to say (CP, p. 139), can endow a thing with properties that it has not already got – apart from the one property of signifying something.

According to the formalist theory, one could not say that $1/2 = 3/6$. For if both expressions are merely shapes, they are not the same shape, but quite different ones. Of course, if one takes them to be signs for contents, the equation states that both signs have the same content. But if no content is present, the equation makes no sense.

The lecture on formal theories really adds little to what is contained in the *Foundations*. But at the beginning of the 1890s Frege published three papers which set out the central theses of his metaphysics and philosophy of language, bringing out what was latent, and clarifying what was confused, in his earlier works.

The first of these is 'Function and Concept' (1891). The notion of function was used in *Concept Script*, but the explanation given there was, as we have seen in Chapter 2, unclear and inconsistent. In the *Foundations* the word is hardly used: it is concepts, not functions, that play a crucial role in the definition of number. In 'Function and Concept' Frege brings the two notions together: it turns out that a concept is a special kind of function.

The notion of function is taken from mathematics, particularly from analysis. But, Frege says, if you ask a mathematician what a function means, you are likely to be given an unsatisfactory answer. 'A function of x is an expression containing x, a formula containing the letter x.' Thus, for instance, '$2 \times 2^2 + 2$' would be a function of 2. This answer will not do, Frege says, because it confuses form and content, sign and thing signified: it has the defects which, as we have just seen, Frege denounced in the formalists (CP, p. 38). But we have also seen that when Frege first introduced the notion of function in *Concept Script*, he too did so in such a way that a function turned out to be an expression of a particular kind, rather than what an expression of that kind signified. Possibly Frege is being coyly self-critical when he says that the confusion between signifier and signified is a mistake 'that is very often met with in mathematical works, even those of celebrated authors'.

The essential thing is not the expression, but its signification or content; not, for instance, the expression '$2 \times 2^2 + 2$', but what it signifies. Well, what does it signify? The same as what is signified by '10'. An equation such as '$2 \times 2^2 + 2 = 10$' means that the right-hand complex of signs has the same signification as the left-hand complex. (Here, as in *Foundations*, Frege holds that an equation states an identity, not a mere likeness or equality: difference of signifier can never be sufficient ground for difference of signified.) Different expressions, appearing on different sides of a true equation, correspond to different notions and aspects but not to different objects.

If a function, as Frege now understands it, is not an expression or any part of an expression, shall we say instead that it is what the expression signifies? That will not do as it stands either: for an expression like '$2(3^2 + 3)$' simply stands for a number. So if a function were merely what a mathematical expression signifies, it would just be a number; and so, as Frege says, by the introduction of functions 'nothing new would have been gained for arithmetic'. The expression '$2x^2 + x$' is more the kind of thing people have in mind when they think of a function; but that expression does not designate a function, but rather indefinitely indicates a number, in the way that 'x' itself does (CP, p. 140).

However, people sometimes call the 'x' in such an expression the *argument* of the function, and this shows us the way to understand the notion of function. In the expressions

$$2 \times 1^2 + 1$$
$$2 \times 4^2 + 4$$
$$2 \times 5^2 + 5$$

we can recognize the same function occurring over and over again, but with different arguments, namely 1, 4 and 5. The content which is common to these expressions is what the function is. It can be represented by '$2(\ )^2 + (\ )$', that is, by what is left of '$2x^2 + x$' if we leave the 'x's out.[1]

The argument is not a part of the function, rather it combines with the function to make a complete whole. A mathematical expression splits into two parts, a sign for an argument and an expression for a function. A function itself is something incomplete, 'unsaturated' as Frege says, and thus it differs fundamentally from a number, which, as he has insisted since the *Foundations*, is a self-subsistent object. The incompleteness of the underlying function is indicated by the occurrence of gaps in the expression for the functions. We may go further than Frege here and call a gappy expression of this kind a 'linguistic function'; for the *Concept Script* has shown that sentences, no less than what sentences signify, can be split into argument and function. Throughout his life Frege used the word 'unsaturated' to describe both functions and function-signs.[2]

1. I am here adapting Frege's text to make it consistent with his current thesis that a function is a matter not of signs but of things signified. What Frege in fact says is: 'the particular essence of function is contained in the common element of these expressions' – such a common element would itself be something linguistic. Just as, in the *Concept Script*, he sometimes lapsed into speaking of non-linguistic functions when officially he was speaking of linguistic functions, so here he lapses into speaking of linguistic functions when officially he is speaking of non-linguistic functions (see p. 26 above, footnote 5).

2. Thus, for instance, in his 1904 paper 'What is a Function?' he writes: 'the sign for a function is "unsaturated"; it needs to be completed with a numeral ... The

Having introduced the notions of function and argument, Frege now introduces the notion of *value*. Mathematicians, Frege says, sometimes say that when two variables x and y are correlated by a law then y is a function of x. But this is an unfortunate way of speaking. A better way to put the matter is that y is the value of a certain function for x as argument. Frege gives the name 'the value of a function for an argument' to the result of completing that function with the argument in question. Thus, for example, 3 is the value of the function $2x^2 + x$ for the argument 1, since we have $2 \times 1^2 + 1 = 3$.

The value of a mathematical function, like its arguments, is always a number; the value of the function is the number which is signified by the whole expression. In a parallel way, according to the theory of linguistic functions in *Concept Script*, the value of a functional expression for a given numeral as argument will be a name or designation of a number. The parallel between signifier and signified is exact.

We can represent the values of a function for different arguments by drawing a graph. The equation '$y = x^2 - 4x$' corresponds to a parabola in which, it would ordinarily be said, 'x' indicates the value of the abscissa, or independent variable, and 'y' indicates the value of the ordinate, or dependent variable. Frege modifies this terminology, and says that 'x' indicates the argument, and 'y' indicates the value of the function.

Frege now introduces an important new notion: that of the *value-range* of a function. If we compare the function $x^2 - 4x$ with the function $x(x-4)$ we find that they always have the same value for the same argument; the same line on a graph corresponds to both functions. In general, whatever x may be,

$$x^2 - 4x = x(x-4)$$

Where this holds, Frege says, the value-ranges of the two functions are identical. In this equation, Frege says,

---

peculiarity of functional signs, which we here called "unsaturatedness", naturally has something answering to it in the functions themselves' (CP, pp. 290–92).

we have not put one function equal to the other, but only the values of one equal to those of the other. And if we so understand this equation that it is to hold whatever argument may be substituted for x, then we have thus expressed that an equation holds generally. But we can also say: 'the value-range of the function $x(x-4)$ is identical with that of the function $x^2 - 4x$' and here we have an identity between ranges of values. (CP, p. 142.)

In this difficult passage, Frege is comparing and contrasting three different but related statements.

The first statement is this:

The function $x(x-4)$ is the same function as $x^2 - 4x$.

Frege says this statement is untrue. We cannot say that the two functions are identical, even though, for the same argument, each function always delivers the same value as the other.

The second is this:

Whatever x may be, $x^2 - 4x = x(x-4)$.

This, as Frege says, states that a certain equation holds generally: it states that x has a certain property (falls under a certain concept), no matter what number x may be. Within the realm of mathematics, this generalized equation presupposes no kinds of entities other than objects (numbers) and their properties.

The third is this:

The two functions, $x(x-4)$ and $x^2 - 4x$, have an identical value-range.

This goes beyond the content of the second statement: it introduces a new metaphysical item, the value-range, which is regarded by Frege as a self-subsistent object like a number. In support of this further step Frege says only:

The possibility of regarding an equation holding generally between values of functions as an identity between ranges of values is, I think, indemonstrable: it must be taken to be a fundamental law of logic. (CP, p. 142.)

Frege introduces a new notation, involving Greek letters, to distinguish the identity of two value-ranges from the generalization of the equation between the values of a function. The latter would normally be expressed, in the modern equivalent of Frege's notation, by

$$(x)\,(x^2 - 4x = x(x - 4))$$

The former in Frege's notation is expressed by

$$\grave{\varepsilon}(\varepsilon^2 - 4\varepsilon) = \grave{\alpha}(\alpha(\alpha - 4)).$$

It cannot be said that Frege makes it altogether clear here what kind of thing a value-range is. Suppose we take the function $y = 2x$. If, as Frege says, the value-range of this function is to be compared with the curve on a graph, then we should expect it to be a set of ordered pairs, thus

$$1, 2.$$
$$2, 4.$$
$$3, 6.$$

and so on.

It is this set of pairs that will be geometrically represented by a graph in which each of the first members of the pairs appears as an abscissa and each of the second members of the pairs appears as an ordinate. Two functions which are representable by the same curves on a graph will have the same value-ranges.

There is nothing problematic, or controversial, about this in itself. As an interpretation of Frege, however, it is problematic because, as we shall see, his later writing suggests a rather different account of value-ranges.[3] What is most controversial about the introduction of value-ranges is Frege's insistence that a value-range, like a number, is a self-subsistent object. As we shall see, in this insistence he was storing up trouble for himself.

*

3. The comparison between value-ranges and a graph recurs in section 36 of *Grundgesetze der Arithmetik*, but it is used for a rather different purpose there.

Just as a variable x, according to Frege, indicates a number indefinitely, so too we can indicate a function indefinitely, for example by the letters 'f' or 'F'. Commonly people write '$f(x)$', or '$F(x)$', where 'x' replaces the argument. But what really indicates the function, and expresses its unsaturated nature, is the fact that a letter like 'F' carries with it a pair of parentheses, containing a gap.[4]

Frege observes that mathematicians are constantly extending the meaning of the word 'function', both by introducing new operations to construct functions, and by introducing new possible arguments and values for functions, for instance, complex numbers.

Frege's own use of 'function' involves a further, and much more fundamental, extension of the notion. He had already made the extension in the *Concept Script* (CN, p. 129), allowing, in addition to signs like ' $+$ ' and ' $-$ ', which serve to construct functional expressions in mathematics, verbs such as 'killed' or 'is lighter than'. In this new context, he makes a rather smoother transition from the mathematical use to the universal use by beginning with verbs that are mathematical symbols, such as ' $=$ ', ' $\geq$ ' or ' $\leq$ '. Let us consider, then, the function $x^2 = 1$.

The first question that arises here is what the values of this function are for different arguments. Now if we replace x successively by $-1, 0, 1, 2$ we get:

$$(-1)^2 = 1,$$
$$0^2 = 1,$$
$$1^2 = 1,$$
$$2^2 = 1.$$

Of these equations the first and third are true, the others false. I say: 'the value of our function is a truth-value' and distinguish between the

---

4. Later, Frege began to use Greek lower-case consonant letters, such as the letter ξ, in informal discussion to indicate the gap in an unsaturated linguistic function, in contradistinction to the italic x, which indefinitely indicates the argument of a saturated function.

truth-values of what is true and what is false. I call the first, for short, the True; and the second the False. (CP, p. 144.)

In the mathematical case, the functional expression, completed by a symbol for an argument, becomes an expression which signifies the value of the function for that argument. If we are to treat $x^2 = 1$ as a function, then '$1^2 = 1$' will be an expression which signifies the value of that function for the argument 1. This is, on Frege's proposal, the truth-value True. So '$1^2 = 1$' will signify the True just as '2^2' signifies 4.

Moreover, in mathematics an equation holds true if the symbols which flank the ' = ' sign both signify the same object (that is, the same number). Since, in Frege's extended system, the two expressions '$3 \geq 2$' and '$5 \leq 7$' both signify the True, we have a valid equation of the form:

$$(3 \geq 2) = (5 \leq 7).$$

The page of 'Function and Concept' which we have just paraphrased contains an extraordinary wealth of original and fruitful philosophical ideas, which were to be developed in far-reaching ways not only by Frege himself but also by many other philosophers. But it must be said that this passage is also a masterpiece of philosophical insouciance. The reader waits anxiously for an explanation of what kind of thing a truth-value is. It is hard to repress an instinctive feeling that the equals sign should stand only between numerals, or at the very most between names, and that it cannot be given this extraordinary new sense by simple fiat. The reader is told only that the broadening of the notion of function is necessary if arithmetic is to be shown to be a development of logic (CP, p. 145). For the present, however, no explanation is given of the nature of truth-value, and nothing is done to palliate the incongruity of equation-signs being used to link whole sentences.

Instead, Frege puts into the reader's mouth a quite different objection. The reader is supposed to object, not to the very idea of sentences being attached to equals signs, but to the possibility of two different sentences being attached to the same equals sign; '3≥2' and '5≤7' express different thoughts, so how can they be joined to make a true equation?

In response, Frege introduces his celebrated distinction between an expression's sense and an expression's reference. Suppose we are asked: Does '2 × 2' mean the same as '12 ÷ 3'? We may be uncertain how to reply. On the one hand, we may want to say that the meaning is different, since the two expressions are constructed in different ways from different elements, and since they represent different operations on different numbers. On the other hand, we may want to say that the meaning of both expressions is the same, namely, the number 4. In order to do justice to both considerations, Frege proposes that we say that the expressions have different senses, but the same reference. Henceforth, when we are asked a question about a meaning of an expression, we must ascertain whether the enquiry concerns the sense or the reference; and the answer may be different in the two cases.[5]

Two different sentences may express the same thought, for instance, two sentences in different languages which are an accurate translation of each other. Again, the same sentence, in different circumstances, may express two different thoughts. A sentence such as 'I am hungry' may be true in one person's mouth and false in another's; and this shows that two different thoughts are being expressed by the same sentence (*Grundgesetze der Arithmetik*, p. 14). This, Frege says, is because 'I' has a different reference in each case. But in general, whether two expressions express the same thought depends not on reference but on sense.

Now '2^2' and '2 + 2' both have the same reference, but they have different senses, and accordingly the sentences '$2^2 = 4$' and

5. To indicate what (following many other authors) I have called 'reference', Frege uses the same German word as he used quite generally prior to 1891 for 'meaning' or 'signification'. His thought can be presented more clearly if a different word is used, and if sense and reference are treated as two different kinds of meaning.

'2 + 2 = 4' express different thoughts. The sense of a sentence is the thought which is its content, and that in turn is determined by the senses of the constituent parts of the sentence. The reference of a sentence is its truth-value: the reference of all true sentences is the True, and the reference of all false sentences is the False. Here again, we encounter a spectacular philosophical innovation, and for the present we wait, open-mouthed but in vain, for an adequate justification.

In the present context Frege is more anxious to develop than to justify his philosophical theses. From sameness of reference, he continues, there does not in general follow sameness of thought.

If we say 'The Evening Star is a planet with a shorter period of revolution than the Earth', the thought we express is other than in the sentence 'The Morning Star is a planet with a shorter period of revolution than the Earth', for somebody who did not know that the Morning Star is the Evening Star might regard one as true and the other as false. (CP, p. 145.)

Two sentences with parts which have the same reference as each other do not necessarily express the same thought; equally, two sentences which are each true (and therefore on Frege's proposal have the same reference) do not necessarily express the same thought.

However, whether an equation holds true depends not on the sense of the expressions which flank the equals sign, but on their reference. Thus '$2^2 = 2 + 2$' is a correct equation, since the reference of each of the flanking expressions is the same, namely the number 4. Similarly, if we are to allow that sentences have truth-values which are their references, 'The Evening Star is a planet = The Morning Star is a planet' will be a correct equation. Both sentences, Frege says, must have the same reference, 'for it is just a matter of interchanging the words "Evening Star" and "Morning Star", which have the same reference, i.e. are proper names of the same heavenly body'.

In *The Foundations of Arithmetic* Frege had spoken not of functions but of concepts. He now links the two notions together. The value of the function $x^2 = 1$ is always one of the truth-values. For the argument -1, its value is the True; we can express this by saying that -1 falls under the concept *square root of 1*. Thus a concept can be exhibited as a certain kind of function: a function whose value is always a truth-value. Thus any predicate, formed by deleting a proper name from a sentence, will express a concept; but a functional expression such as 'the capital of . . .' will not, since the value of the corresponding function for an appropriate argument – for example, France – will be not a truth-value but a city, for example, Paris (CP, p. 147).

If two functions always have the same values for the same arguments, they have the same value-ranges. This will hold of functions which are concepts in the same way as it holds of other functions. We are now in a position to define the extension of a concept as its value-range. As Frege puts it, we can designate as an extension the value-range of a function whose value for every argument is a truth-value.

The notion of extension presented here appears, on the face of it, to be quite different from that in the *Foundations*. There the notion of extension was presented without explanation, and it was to be assumed that it was the notion used by logicians prior to Frege, according to which the extension of a concept is given by the objects falling under it: thus the extension of the concept *horse* would be all the horses there are.[6] On the new notion, as we have interpreted it earlier in this chapter, the extension of the concept would be a series of pairs, with one member of each pair being a truth-value, and the other member being an object.

6. Or, perhaps the set of all horses. But the difference is slight since most logicians before Frege thought of a set as given by the enumeration of its members. In any case, even in the *Foundations* Frege attributes extension to empty concepts, so he was not misled by the confusions of his predecessors (see p. 88 above).

Objects which are, in fact, horses would be paired with the True, and objects which are not horses would be paired with the False, so that the extension of the concept would go like this:

Bucephalus:	the True,
Alexander:	the False,
Eclipse:	the True,
Julius Caesar:	the False,
. . .	. . .,
. . .	. . .,

and so on. Given that the number of the number of objects in the universe is constant, the extension of every concept will be of the same size; the extensions of different concepts, if they differ, will differ only in the different pairings.

A clear advantage of this notion of extension, by comparison with the traditional notion, is that it gives every concept an extension. Given the traditional explanation, it was difficult to see how a concept such as *unicorn* or *not identical with itself* had an extension at all, since no objects fall under such a concept. But on the explanation suggested by the comparison between a value-range and a curve on a graph, the extension of such concepts is exactly the same kind of thing as the extension of any ordinary concept; the only difference is that every pair in the extension will have as its second member the False.

Frege, having concentrated so far in 'Function and Concept' on mathematical examples, now moves to consider statements of all kinds, as he did in *Concept Script*.

We split up the sentence 'Caesar conquered Gaul' into 'Caesar' and 'conquered Gaul'. The second part is 'unsaturated' – it contains an empty place; only when this place is filled up with a proper name, or with an expression that replaces a proper name, does a complete sense appear. (CP, pp. 146–7.)

But instead of using the word 'function' to denote the unsaturated part of the sentence, as he did in *Concept Script*, he now says 'I give the name "Function" to what this unsaturated part stands for.' And he gives as the argument not 'Caesar' but Caesar.

Arguments of functions, therefore, are not now names but objects. Numbers are not the only objects that can appear as arguments of functions; so too can persons, cities, truth-values, value-ranges of functions, extensions of concepts and objects of any kind whatever. What then is an object? Frege regards the notions as too simple to be analysed. 'I can only say briefly: an object is anything that is not a function, so that an expression for it does not contain any empty place.' (CP, p. 147.)

Once we extend the possible range of arguments, we need to define our existing function-signs in new possible contexts. Scientific rigour demands, Frege says, that we guard against any sign coming to lack meaning; thus we need to define the plus sign not only between integers, but also between objects of any kind whatever.

It is thus necessary to lay down rules from what it follows e.g. what
$$\odot + 1$$
is to mean, if ' $\odot$ ' means the Sun. What rules we lay down is a matter of comparative indifference; but is essential that we should do so – that '$a + b$' should always have a reference, whatever signs for definite objects may be inserted in place of 'a' and 'b'. (CP, p. 148.)

This is to satisfy Frege's requirement that any concept must be sharply delimited: it must be determinable, for any object, whether or not it falls under the concept.

Frege now introduces the assertion sign, the sign for negation, the universal quantifier and the way in which these can be used to express generalizations and existential statements. He does so in much the same way as he did in *Concept Script*, with this difference, that the rules are now stated in terms of the theory that the reference of a proposition is a truth-value. Thus, instead of saying that the universal quantifier in $(x) \Phi (x)$ signifies that the function is a fact whatever we take its argument to be, he now says that the sign '$(x) \Phi (x)$' stands for the True when the function $\Phi (x)$ has the True as its value whatever the argument.

The assertion sign is now explained as asserting that what follows it designates the True.

Second-level functions (which correspond to what were called 'second-order concepts' in *Foundations*) are introduced in 'Function and Concept' in the following manner. The expression '$\neg(x)\neg f(x)$' can be looked on as expressing a function whose argument is the function indicated by 'f'. A statement to the effect that there are black swans ascribes the property of existence (more strictly, of being instantiated) to the concept *black swan*; since a concept is a function, here we have a function (*. . . is a black swan*) appearing as an argument of a second-level function (*has an object falling under it*).

Just as functions are fundamentally different from objects, so also functions whose arguments are and must be functions are fundamentally different from functions whose arguments are objects and cannot be anything else. (CP, p. 153.)

Frege goes on to introduce, as he has done since *Concept Script*, first-level functions of two arguments, such as $x^2 + y^2$ and $x^2 + y^2 = 9$. The second of these two examples, unlike the first, is a function whose value is always a truth-value. First-level two-argument functions of this kind Frege calls relations.

Among second-level functions we must now, accordingly, distinguish between those which take one-argument functions as their arguments, and those that take two-argument functions as their arguments. Properties of relations are second-level functions which take two-argument functions as their argument.

For instance, a relation is symmetrical if whenever one thing has the relation to another, that other thing also has the relation to the first thing. (The relations *spouse of* and *sibling of* are symmetrical; the relations *husband of* and *sister of* are not.) In symbols:

$$(x)(y)(F(x, y) \to F(y, x))$$

In this formula the letter 'F' indicates the argument, and the two places, separated by a comma, with the parentheses that follow

'F' are to show that 'F' represents a function with two arguments. Symmetry, then, is a second-level function of first-level functions with two arguments.

The recognition of second-level functions, Frege says, marks a culminating step in a progress of increasing arithmetical sophistication. First people did calculations with individual numbers; then they moved to algebraic letters; then they recognized first-level functions and introduced functional variables; finally, we have reached second-level functions.

One might think that this would go on. but probably the last step is already not so rich in consequences as the earlier ones; for instead of second-level functions one can deal, in further advances, with first-level functions – as shall be shown elsewhere. (CP, p. 156.)

This was an announcement of the programme, to be carried out in *Grundgesetze der Arithmetik*, of using value-ranges, instead of concepts, as the fundamental items in the construction of arithmetic.

The paper 'Concept and Object' of 1892 takes as its starting point a controversy between Frege and another mathematician who had reviewed *The Foundations of Arithmetic*. The main point at issue was whether one and the same item could be both concept and object. Frege had emphatically denied this; his reviewer had said that such a thing was no odder than a person's being both a father and a son. Frege replied:

Let us fasten on this simile! If there were, or had been, beings that were fathers but could not be sons, such beings would obviously be quite different in kind from all men who are sons. Now it is something like this that happens here. (CP, p. 183.)

The application of the simile is not immediately obvious. As the argument proceeds it seems that Frege is, for the moment, conceding that perhaps concepts can also be objects, while rejecting entirely the idea that objects can also be concepts. Concepts, on that interpretation, would be the analogues of ordinary human beings; objects would be like fathers who could not be sons. In the analogy, to be a son is to be predicative.

'The concept', Frege says, 'is predicative.' This is in accord with his teaching in the *Foundations* and in 'Function and Concept'. In all the writings we have considered there is clearly a special relationship between a concept and a predicate; but what exactly the relationship is remains unclear. Is a concept identical with a predicate? Is it the sense of a predicate? Is it its reference? The fuller explanation given in 'Concept and Object' is supposed to cast light on the earlier writings and help us to answer questions such as these. In fact, it raises more questions than it answers.

Let us look back to *The Foundations of Arithmetic*. A footnote on p. 77 of that work reads as follows:

A concept is for me that which can be the predicate of a singular judgement-content, an object that which can be the subject of the same. If in the proposition

The direction of the axis of the telescope is identical
with the direction of the Earth's axis

we take the direction of the axis of the telescope as subject, then the predicate is 'identical with the direction of the Earth's axis'. This is a concept. (FA, p. 77.)

This footnote is not easy to interpret. A predicate is most naturally taken to be a piece of language, and this interpretation may seem to be confirmed by Frege's use of quotation marks to introduce his instance of a predicate. However, in his early works Frege uses quotation marks to indicate what predicates signify, as well as the predicates themselves, even in passages where he is quite clearly distinguishing between signs and what they signify.[7] In the present passage, a predicate is an element of a judgeable content, and that belongs to the realm not of the

---

7. In my exposition of him hitherto I have made use of the convention which he himself introduced in 'Concept and Object' of using italics for the concept, and reserving quotation marks for linguistic items.

signifier, but of the signified. Frege surely does not mean here that a concept is a piece of language; rather, it is something that in some way lies behind language.

In 'Concept and Object' Frege admits that there was confusion in the wording of the footnote in the *Foundations*. However, his recantation compounds the obscurity. He says

> When I wrote my *Foundations of Arithmetic* I had not yet made the distinction between sense and reference; and so, under the expression 'a possible content of judgement', I was combining what I now designate by the distinctive words 'thought' and 'truth-value'. (CP, p. 187.)

Two things are puzzling here. First, the confusion in the *Foundations* seemed to be between a sign and its signification; but here the confusion is identified as that between sense and reference, both of which are forms of signification. Secondly, the distinction between thought and truth-value concerns the signification of a complete sentence: whereas the issue needing clarification concerns the signification of a (grammatical) predicate.

Frege now restates his view, which, he says, remains still essentially the same. He does so in the following terms.

> We may say in brief, taking 'subject' and 'predicate' in the linguistic sense: A concept is the reference of a predicate; an object is something that can never be the whole reference of a predicate, but can be the reference of a subject. (CP, p. 187.)

This is an important passage. 'Function and Concept' had left it uncertain whether a concept was the sense, or the reference, of a predicate. On the one hand, Frege says that a function is what the unsaturated part of a sentence stands for, using the verb appropriate for reference (CP, p. 146). On the other hand, he also says that a function-symbol *expresses* a function, and this is the verb he commonly uses, in both his earlier and later writings, to signify the relation between a sign and its sense.[8]

---

8. See, most explicitly, *Grundgesetze der Arithmetik*, 35: 'I say further that what a name *expresses* is its sense, and what it *stands for* is its reference.'

If we are to talk of the reference of a predicate, the value-range of a concept might have seemed to be more appropriate to be such a reference than the concept itself. However, here in 'Concept and Object', and in a number of later passages, Frege is quite explicit that the concept is the reference, not the sense, of the predicate.

If a concept is the reference of a predicate, what, we may ask, is the sense of the predicate? Some passages in Frege give the impression that there is no answer to this question and that a predicate has no sense. But if so, what is the point, in the case of the predicate, of making a distinction between sense and reference? Only in unpublished writings is there a clear answer to the question: just as a predicate is an unsaturated part of a sentence, the sense of a predicate is an unsaturated part of the thought which is the sense of the sentence.[9]

However, here Frege is principally interested not in determining the sense and reference of predicates, but in contrasting predicates with proper names. A proper name, he says, is quite incapable of being used as a grammatical predicate.

To illustrate this point of Frege's we may consider the two propositions:

(1)   Charlotte Brontë was a writer of books,
(2)   Charlotte Brontë was Currer Bell.

At first sight it looks as if 'was Currer Bell' is a predicate on all fours with 'was a writer of books', and thus provides a counter-example to the thesis that a proper name cannot be used as a predicate. But this, Frege says, involves a misunderstanding of the verb 'to be'.

---

9. This is most clearly stated in the posthumously published 'Introduction to Logic' written in 1906. Having said that sentences express thoughts, and that sentences also have, in addition to complete parts (proper names), unsaturated parts, he goes on to say, 'The unsaturated part of the thought we take to be a sense too: it is the sense of the part of the sentence over and above the proper name' (PW, p. 192).

In the first example, 'was' is a simple copula, a mark of predication: this is clear from the fact that (1) is synonymous with

(3)   Charlotte Brontë wrote books.

This is a sentence which states that Charlotte Bronte falls under the concept *wrote books*, and the copula has quite disappeared. In (2), by contrast, the verb 'to be' functions as the mark of an equation or identity, just like the ' = ' sign. So (2) is synonymous with

(4)   Charlotte Brontë = Currer Bell.

This is a sentence ascribing two different proper names to one and the same individual. Note that (3) and (4) are sentences of quite different types: an equation is reversible, while an object's falling under a concept is a relation that is irreversible.

The name, or pseudonym, 'Currer Bell' does not figure as a predicate in (2) or (4); it is only a part of the predicate. This could be brought out by rewriting (2) as

(5)   Charlotte Brontë was none other than Currer Bell.

where 'none other than Currer Bell' will be said by Frege to stand for a concept, a concept under which only one object falls.

A general criterion which Frege gives for distinguishing between concepts and objects is that the singular definite article always indicates an object, while the indefinite article accompanies a concept-word. German and English usage are sufficiently close together for this criterion to be no less and no more plausible in one language than in the other.

Frege says that there are hardly any exceptions to the thesis about the indefinite article. Sentences such as 'A man is sitting in the waiting-room' or 'Schopenhauer bought a dog' are, for Frege, only apparent counter-examples. Each sentence tells us that there is some object that falls under a concept, in the first case the concept *man sitting in the waiting room* and in the

119

second case the concept *dog bought by Schopenhauer*. In each case the word accompanied by the indefinite article turns out to correspond to one of the components of the concept.

With regard to the singular definite article, the only exception that Frege recognizes is the case where a singular term can be regarded as standing for a plural. He considers two such cases. In 'The Turk besieged Vienna', he says, 'The Turk' is obviously the proper name of a people; while 'The horse is a four-legged animal' expresses a universal judgement to the effect that all horses are four-legged animals.

The words 'all', 'any', 'no', 'some', like the word 'a', belong grammatically with concept-words, not with proper names. But in sentences such as

(6)   All mammals are land-dwellers

what we are really doing is expressing relations between concepts. Accordingly, the words belong not with the particular concept-words which immediately follow them, but with the sentence considered as a whole. This, of course, is what happens if we replace these words of ordinary language with the quantifier notation of *Concept Script*.

Ordinary language gives the impression that 'all mammals' is the logical subject of a sentence like (6). This impression is quite illusory, as we can show easily if we consider negation. If 'All mammals' were the subject of (6), then its negation would be

(7)   All mammals are not land-dwellers

instead of being, as it obviously is,

(8)   Not all mammals are land-dwellers

Like the quantifier-words listed above, the expression 'There is a . . .' or 'There exists a . . .', belongs with concepts, not with objects. These are all expressions which cannot be sensibly attached to the names of objects. 'There is Julius Caesar', for Frege, is neither true nor false, but senseless; and no well-formed sentence could contain the expressions 'all Julius Caesars' or 'some Julius Caesars'. If in a genuine sentence one of these quantifying expressions is attached to what looks like a proper name, then we can be sure that what we are dealing with is in fact a disguised concept-word. It is thus that Frege deals with the sentences 'Trieste is no Vienna' and 'There is only one Vienna': in each of these instances 'Vienna' is being used as a concept-word, equivalent perhaps to 'city like Vienna'.

Frege's criteria for distinguishing between concepts and objects are essentially grammatical criteria for distinguishing concept-expressions from object-words. To the objection that logical rules cannot be based on linguistic distinctions, Frege replies that logical rules cannot be stated without appeal to the understanding of natural language, and that what he is offering are not formal definitions, but only hints designed to elicit understanding. No formal language could take the place of ordinary language in communicating this understanding; because only a person who could already distinguish in ordinary language between names and predicates would ever be able to translate correctly into a formal language.

The principal contention of 'Concept and Object' is that there is an unbridgeable gulf between concepts and objects, such that what can sensibly be said of the one cannot sensibly be said of the other. Objects can fall under concepts; concepts cannot do so. Frege, having made this claim, lists objections to it, and answers the objections in turn.

(i) Concepts can surely have properties: and to have a property is to fall under a concept.

Frege did indeed assert in *The Foundations of Arithmetic*, and repeats here, that concepts have properties, and concepts have relationships to each other. Such cases fall into two different groups.

(a) One first-level concept can be subordinate to another first-level concept. Thus, the concept *mammal* is subordinate to the concept *animal*; *animal* is a component of the concept *mammal*, but it is not a property of it. However, both *animal* and *mammal*

121

are properties of, say, Lord Emsworth's pig, the Empress of Blandings; that is to say, the Empress of Blandings falls under both concepts (CP, p. 190).

(b) A first-level concept may fall under a second-level concept. Thus a concept may have properties such as being instantiated, or having four objects fall under it. For instance, the sentence

> The concept *square root of 4* is instantiated

attributes to the concept in question the property of instantiation, which is the same as saying it falls under a second-level concept *instantiated*. Frege says here:

The relation of an object to a first-level concept that it falls under is different from the (admittedly similar) relation of a first-level to a second-level concept. (To do justice at once to the distinction and to the similarity we might perhaps say: An object falls *under* a first-level concept; a concept falls *within* a second-level concept.) (CP, p. 190.)

(ii) Frege had laid down as a grammatical criterion to distinguish object from concept that a definite article preceding an expression was a sure indication that the expression which followed designated an object, not a concept. If we accept this criterion, we will be puzzled how to construe the following sentence:

(9)   The concept *horse* is a concept easily attained.

Because the expression 'the concept *horse*' begins with a definite article, it must, by Frege's criterion, refer to an object. On the other hand, because of its content, it must surely refer to a concept. So the criterion for distinguishing concept and object breaks down.

Frege's response to this problem is robust. He embraces the first horn of the dilemma. He agrees that the three words 'the concept *horse*' do designate an object, but on that very account, he says, they do not designate a concept (CP, p. 184). He admits that this is slightly embarrassing: the city of Berlin is a city, and the volcano Vesuvius is a volcano; why therefore is not the concept *horse* a concept? It is nothing more, however, Frege claims, than an unavoidable awkwardness of natural language.

> In logical discussions one quite often needs to assert something about a concept, and to express this in the form usual for such assertions – viz. to make what is asserted of the concept into the content of the grammatical predicate. Consequently, one would expect that the reference of the grammatical subject would be the concept; but the concept as such cannot play this part, in view of its predicative nature; it must first be converted into an object, or, speaking more precisely, an object must go proxy for it. (CP, p. 186. cf. BLA, p. 37.)

Frege makes a distinction between 'the concept *F*' when it occurs as a grammatical subject and when it occurs within a grammatical predicate. If such an expression occurs within a grammatical predicate, then we have simply a circumlocution; for instance,

(10)   Jesus falls under the concept *man*

says no more and no less than

(11)   Jesus is a man.

But no such simple reduction is possible where 'the concept *F*' occurs in the subject place.

Even commentators who are very sympathetic to Frege are reluctant to defend him on this point. They have found it difficult to swallow his contention that the concept *horse* is not a concept. At best, they say, he should have defended himself against his critics by saying that any sentence whose grammatical subject is 'The concept . . .' is ill formed. He should not have admitted that 'The concept *horse* is a concept' can be false; it is just a nonsense.

It is my belief that Frege's critics are making unnecessary difficulties here, and that Frege himself, in a footnote in 'Concept and Object', provided ample justification for his contention that the concept *horse* is not a concept. He wrote:

A similar thing happens when we say as regards the sentence 'this rose is red': The grammatical predicate 'is red' belongs to the subject 'this rose'. Here the words 'the grammatical predicate "is red"' are not a grammatical predicate but a subject. By the very act of explicitly calling it a predicate, we deprive it of this property. (CP, p. 186.)

Suppose that we wish to assign the word 'swims' to a grammatical category. We might try to do so first by writing

(12)   swims is a verb,

but this produces not a sentence, but an ungrammatical concatentation of words. The correct way to do so is to write

(13)   'swims' is a verb.

Few people, I think, would regard this sentence as anything but true. But of course, the expression which appears as the subject of that sentence is not a verb, but a name, formed by placing quotation marks round the verb. None the less, the sentence

(14)   'swims' is a name

is quite false. But there is nothing mysterious about this, any more than there is anything mysterious about the fact that while 'Julius Caesar' is a name, the sentence

(15)   Julius Caesar is a name

is false.

The relation between ξ *is a horse* and the concept *horse* is to be understood on the basis of this parallel. If we write

(16) ξ *is a horse* is not a concept

we do not produce a sentence, but a piece of nonsense.

If we write, however,

(17)   the concept *horse* is not a concept,

we have something which is not necessarily nonsense, but which can be understood in more than one way.

Consider the following sentences:

(18)   the verb 'swims' is not a verb,
(19)   'the verb "swims"' is not a verb,
(20)   the verb '"swims"' is not a verb,

Of these three sentences, (18) is clearly false and (19) is clearly true; while (20) gives us pause for thought. It is certainly true that '"swims"' is not a verb, but this is not quite what the third sentence says. We are reluctant to say that the third sentence is true, because the single quotation marks are preceded by the misleading expression 'the verb'. I believe that it is the third sentence which is the key to the understanding of Frege's contention that the concept *horse* is not a concept. The expression 'the concept . . .' is really meant to serve the same purpose with regard to concepts which quotation marks serve in relation to predicates. That is the main function of the expression; and if the expression is so understood, then the sentence 'the concept horse is not a concept' is undoubtedly true, just as

(21)   '"swims"' is not a verb

is true. But the expression 'the concept *horse*' is constructed on the model of the misleading expression 'the verb '"swims"'' in (20) above; and that is why Frege's critics have pounced upon it. But Frege himself regards this as simply an awkwardness of language, no more to be taken seriously when we are dealing with logic than the difference between 'and' and 'but', or between 'dog' and 'cur'. Accordingly, it seems to me, Frege is justified in saying that the sentence 'the concept *horse* is not a concept' provides no counter-example to his contention that a gulf is fixed between objects and concepts.

CHAPTER 7

SENSE AND REFERENCE

The distinction between sense and reference first presented in 'Function and Concept' in 1891 was developed in another paper which was written in conjunction with it, although it was not published until 1892. This second paper, 'Sense and Reference', presents arguments for, and answers objections to, some of the more puzzling theses which were baldly stated in the earlier paper.

The paper starts by asking a question about identity. Is identity a relation? If it is a relation, is it a relation between objects, or between signs for objects? The second answer suggests itself, because – to take the example used in 'Function and Concept' – 'the morning star = the morning star' is a statement very different in cognitive value from 'the morning star = the evening star'. The former is analytically true, while the second records an astronomical discovery. If we were to regard identity as a relation between what the signs stand for it would seem that if '$a = b$' is true, then '$a = a$' could not differ from '$a = b$'. 'A relation would thereby be expressed of a thing to itself, and indeed one in which each thing stands to itself but to no other thing.' (CP, p. 157.)

It seems natural to conclude, then, that equations express relations between signs, and that '$a = b$' says that the signs 'a' and 'b' designate the same thing. This was the view Frege had adopted in Section 8 of *Concept Script*, where he introduced a sign for identity of content, and said that this signified the circumstance of two names having the same content.

But there is an objection to this view. Names are arbitrary, and if every sentence of the form '$a = b$' really signified a relationship between symbols, it would not express any knowledge about the extra-linguistic world. 'The evening star = the morning star' would record a lexical fact rather than an astronomical fact. This was a point which Frege had already realized at the time of writing *Concept Script*, where he says that the need for having a symbol for equality of content rests on the fact that the same content can be fully determined in different ways (as he illustrates with a geometrical example); and that a synthetic judgement of identity states that the same content is given by two ways of determining it (see p. 33).

In 'Sense and Reference', Frege says that a statement of identity can be informative only if the difference between the signs corresponds to a difference in the mode of presentation of what is designated.

Let a, b, c be the lines connecting the vertices of a triangle with the midpoints of the opposite sides. The point of intersection of a and b is then the same as the point of intersection of b and c. So we have different designations for the same point, and these names ('point of intersection of a and b', 'point of intersection of b and c') likewise indicate the mode of presentation; and hence the statement contains actual knowledge. (CP, p. 158.)

It is this mode of presentation which constitutes the *sense* of the sign. The reference of the two expressions quoted in the passage above is the same, but the sense of each is different.

We can say, then, that an identity statement will be true and informative if the equals sign is flanked by two names with the same reference but different senses. The word 'name' is, as the examples show, being used in a broad sense to include complex designations of objects. Frege is prepared to call all such designations 'proper names'.

In Frege's mature account of meaning there are items at three levels: signs, their senses and their references. Signs, we may say, express their senses and stand for, or denote, their references. By using signs we express a sense and denote a reference (CP, p. 161).

In a well-regulated language, every sign would have a sense, and only one sense. In natural languages, a sign may have more than one sense: a word like 'staff' is ambiguous; the expression 'the dog', if it is to have a precise sense, needs different supplementation in different households; different scholars would give different explanations of the name 'Aristotle'. Frege says that we have to be content if the same word has the same sense in the same context. While in an ideal language there would be only one sense for every sign, there is no requirement, even in an ideal language, that every sense should have only one sign. In the real world the same sense may be expressed by different signs in different languages or even in the same language.

In a good translation, the sense of the original text will be preserved. What is lost in translation is not a matter of sense, but, Frege says, 'the colouring and shading which poetic eloquence seeks to give to the sense'. This is something which is not objective in the way that sense is objective.

Not every sense has a reference corresponding to it. The expressions 'The celestial body most distant from the Earth' and 'The least rapidly convergent series' both have senses, but the former probably, and the latter certainly, lacks a reference and stands for no object. Conversely, one and the same object may be referred to by expressions of quite different senses: this was the starting point for the drawing of the distinction in the first place. If one knew all that there was to know about an object one would know which senses would serve to pick it out and which would not. But of course we humans never attain such knowledge.

The sense of a word is what we grasp when we understand a word. It is quite different from a mental image, even though, if a sign refers to a tangible object, I may well have a mental image associated with it. Images are subjective and vary from person to person, and within the same person from time to time; but the sense of a sign, Frege says, 'may be the common property of many and therefore is not a part of a mode of the individual mind'.

Frege offers an analogy for the relationship between reference, sense and mental image:

Somebody observes the Moon through a telescope. I compare the Moon itself to the reference; it is the object of the observation, mediated by the real image projected by the object glass in the interior of the telescope, and by the retinal image of the observer. The former I compare to the sense, the latter is like the image or experience. The optical image in the telescope is indeed one-sided and dependent upon the standpoint of observation; but it is still objective, inasmuch as it can be used by several observers. It could be arranged for several people to use it simultaneously. But each one would have his own retinal image. (CP, p. 160.)

An image is *my* image or *your* image; but a sense does not, in the same way, have an owner. It is because senses are public and common that thoughts can be passed on from one generation to another.

We know, from 'Function and Concept', that it is not only proper names – simple or complex – that have senses and references. What of entire sentences, which express thoughts? Is the thought, the content of the sentence, the sense or the reference of a sentence?

Let us assume for the time being that the sentence has reference. If we now replace one word of the sentence by another having the same reference, but a different sense, this can have no bearing upon the reference of the sentence. Yet we can see that in such a case the thought changes; since, e.g., the thought in the sentence 'The morning star is a body illuminated by the Sun' differs from that in the sentence 'The evening star is a body illuminated by the Sun'. Anybody who did not know that the evening star is the morning star might hold the one thought to be true, the other false. The thought, accordingly, cannot be the reference of the sentence, but must rather be considered as the sense. (CP, p. 162.)

Frege is clearly operating with a tacit criterion for the identity of thoughts: two thoughts are identical if and only if it is not possible to hold either thought to be true without holding the other one to be true. This suggests a general criterion for the identity of senses: that two senses are the same if and only if it would be impossible to grasp them both without realizing that they determined the same reference. For the truth-value of a proposition is its reference, as we know from 'Function and Concept'.

Here, in 'Sense and Reference', an argument is provided for that earlier assertion.

Is it possible that a sentence as a whole has only a sense, but no reference? At any rate, one might expect that such sentences occur, just as there are parts of sentences having sense but no reference. And sentences which contain proper names without reference will be of this kind. The sentence 'Odysseus was set ashore at Ithaca while sound asleep' obviously has a sense. But since it is doubtful whether the name 'Odysseus', occurring therein, has reference, it is also doubtful whether the whole sentence has one. (CP, p. 162.)

The argument seems to go like this. We must expect that the reference of a sentence is determined by the reference of the parts of a sentence. Let us inquire, therefore, what is missing from a sentence if one of its parts lacks a reference. If we were interested only in the thought, it would not matter to us whether 'Odysseus' has a reference or not, for the thought remains the same in either case, being determined by the senses, not the references, of the constituent parts of the proposition.

It is only if you want seriously to take the sentence as true or as false that you need to ascribe a reference to 'Odysseus'; for if you do not, there will be nothing for the predicate to be true or false of.

Why do we want every proper name to have not only a sense, but also a reference? Why is the thought not enough for us? Because, and to the extent that, we are concerned with its truth value. (CP, p. 163.)

The sense, and the associated images, are sufficient to make us enjoy an epic poem: what pushes us to advance from sense to reference is the attitude of scientific investigation, the striving for truth. We are, therefore, Frege says, driven into accepting as the reference of a sentence its truth-value, the True or, as the case may be, the False. Every seriously propounded indicative sentence is a name of one or other of these objects. All true sentences have the same reference as each other, and so do all false sentences.

Frege's thesis that the relation between a sentence and its truth-value is the same as that between a name and its reference is connected with his general distinction between predication and assertion. It is no doubt more natural to think of the relation between a thought and its truth as being that of subject to predicate: we say, after all, 'The thought that 5 is a prime number is true.' But, Frege says, the thought expressed by that whole sentence is only the same thought as is contained by the simpler sentence '5 is a prime number.' (This is in accord with the tacit criterion for the identity of thoughts mentioned earlier.) These two sentences have the same sense, and both of them are names of the True; but only if they are asserted do they *say that* they are names of the True.

Subject and predicate (understood in the logical sense) are indeed elements of thought; they stand on the same level as items for comprehension. By combining subject and predicate one reaches only a thought, never passes from sense to reference, never from a thought to its truth-value. (CP, p. 164.)

It is by making a judgement, which is not the mere comprehension of a thought, but an acceptance of its truth, that we take the step from the level of thought to the level of reference.

The difference between assertion and predication, in ordinary discourse, is made out by grammatical mood, by context and by convention. In Frege's formal system, as we saw when we were considering *Concept Script*, this difference is supposed to be marked by a special assertion sign.

In the course of Frege's writing, at least two different functions are attributed to the assertion sign. Sometimes the assertion sign is considered as a sign that what follows is seriously meant; that is to say, that it is meant to be taken seriously and not as part of a charade or fiction. At other times, it is taken as being the mark of the assertoric mood, as when it is said that its function is to distinguish an assertion from a supposition or a question.

Frege treats the assertion sign as a sign that what follows is seriously meant when he says that in fiction we are only interested in the sense of sentences and not in their truth-values. Actors on the stage, he says, utter words which are signs having only a sense; the assertion sign, which is used to assert that the reference of what follows it is the True, cannot be used in conjunction with signs that have no reference, and therefore cannot be used by an actor on the stage. The assertion sign, in Frege's thought, seems to be like the sign of the treble clef. The clef shows how each note which follows it is to be read, and so the assertion sign shows that each word following it is to be taken seriously.

But it seems obvious that there is something futile in introducing a sign to denote that a sentence is to be taken seriously. If it was in question whether an ordinary sentence was to be taken seriously, it could equally be questioned whether a sentence preceded by an assertion sign was to be taken seriously. According to Frege, the actor on the stage who says 'the thought that 5 is a prime number is true' no more makes a serious assertion than if he said '5 is a prime number' (CP, p. 164). But, equally, an actor who in the course of a play wrote the sentence preceded by an assertion sign on a blackboard would not have made a serious assertion either.

Whether an utterance is meant seriously is a different question from whether the utterance is in the assertoric mood. The question 'Did you mean that seriously?' can be asked of commands no less than it can be asked of statements. Even in the case of suppositions, which are Frege's favourite examples of sentences which are *not* assertions, there is a difference between an idle fantasy and a hypothesis put forward for exploration.[1]

---

1. I have treated this issue at greater length in my book *Will, Freedom and Power*, pp. 36–8.

There is indeed scope for a sign to mark the difference between the assertoric mood and other moods, and natural languages have such signs in verb inflexions and auxiliary verbs. However, it is not necessary to make use of such a sign in order to expound Frege's system, since in his treatment he explicitly ignores sentences in other than assertoric moods since his overriding aim is to describe, and in part construct, a language which is appropriate for the purposes of theoretical science.

Acceptance of the distinction between assertion and predication, and of the distinction between the assertoric and other moods, does not force us, as Frege seems to think it does, to regard truth-values as the references of sentences. It is true that if a truth-value is an object then it cannot be represented by a predicate (which has to correspond to something unsaturated, like a concept). But the converse is not true.

Frege may be right that '. . . is true' is not a genuine predicate, and does not express any function. But his argument seems to involve two further steps. (1) The only entities in the world that correspond to language are objects and functions, so if truth is not a function it must be an object. (2) The only relation an object can have to language is being the reference of a name; hence truth is something which is named by true sentences. But why cannot there be linguistic items which are neither names nor linguistic functions? Is not Frege's assertion sign itself such an item? And if so, why is '. . . is true' not also such an item?

Some philosophers have thought that for a sentence, or a thought, to be true was for it to correspond to something extra-linguistic and extra-mental: a fact, perhaps, or a state of affairs, or what Frege in *Concept Script* called a circumstance. There are grave difficulties in identifying the facts, or states of affairs, or circumstances, to which true propositions are alleged to correspond: but it is surprising that Frege does not here consider this possibility, even if only to reject it.

Frege talks, not of facts, but of parts of truth-values. But he says:

I have here used 'part' in a special sense. That is, I have transferred to the reference of a sentence the relation between the whole and the parts of a sentence itself, by calling the reference of the word a part of the reference of the sentence, if the word itself is part of the sentence. (CP, p. 165.)

Frege admits that there is something objectionable about this, because 'the whole reference and one part of it do not suffice to determine the reference of the remainder'. Frege continued to worry about this problem, but he did not ever satisfactorily resolve, even in his own mind, the unease here expressed. For the present he contents himself with saying that perhaps a word other than 'part' should be invented.

At the three levels of Frege's system, corresponding to a sentence containing a name, there are three different, but parallel, part–whole relationships, which are of increasing obscurity.

First, at the level of signs, there is the distinction between function and argument within sentences, according to the linguistic function/argument analysis with which the *Concept Script* replaced the traditional distinction between grammatical subject and grammatical predicate. Thus, in the sentence 'Nero fiddled', the parts are the name 'Nero' and the predicate '. . . fiddled'.

Secondly, at the level of sense, there are two elements: the sense of the name involved, and the sense expressed by the predicates: in the case in point, *the fifth Roman Emperor* (or the like), and whatever it is that one grasps when one understands the predicate '. . . fiddled'. These parts constitute the whole, which is a thought, the thought *that Nero fiddled*.

Thirdly, at the level of reference, there is the whole, which is a truth-value, and there is at least one part which Frege identifies, the reference of the name, which in this case is the Emperor Nero himself. In 'Sense and Reference' Frege is very unforthcoming about the other part, 'the remainder'; but we know from 'Concept and Object' that it must be the concept ξ *fiddled*.[2]

---

2. Frege gives a cross-reference (CP, p. 158) to the passage of 'Concept and Object' discussed above at p. 123.

One might have expected that at the level of reference the two parts would be the reference of the name, Nero, and the extension of the concept ξ *fiddled*. But, no doubt for good reason, Frege hesitates to say this. None the less, he proceeds resolutely to make use of the 'part/whole' terminology at the level of reference, and he uses it to support the thesis that the reference of a sentence is its truth-value. If a part of a sentence is replaced by another with the same reference, then the reference of the whole must remain constant. And in fact the truth-value (and probably nothing but the truth-value) of a sentence does remain constant in such a case (CP, p. 164). If, say, in the example above, 'Nero' is replaced by 'The son of the younger Agrippina' the sentence remains true.

The same is true if the expression to be substituted is not a name but a sentence or clause within a proposition. If the reference of a sentence is, as the thesis claims, a truth-value, then the truth-value of a sentence containing another as a part must remain unchanged when the part is replaced by another sentence having the same truth-value.

This is the case, of course, when sentences are joined to each other to make larger sentences by means of conjunctions such as 'and', 'or' and 'if . . . then', if these conjunctions are understood in the manner explained in the *Concept Script* (see p. 27 above). These connectives, so understood, are truth-functional; that is to say, the truth-values of propositions compounded by these connectives depend only on the truth-values, and not on the content, of the propositions so compounded. It will follow that if we take any such compound proposition and replace one of its components with another proposition of different sense but the same truth-value the truth-value of the whole will not alter.

Frege takes here as an example the sentence

If the Sun has already risen, the sky is very cloudy,

and he says of this sentence:

Here it can be said that a relation between the truth-values of conditional and dependent clauses has been asserted, viz. such that the case does not occur in which the antecedent stands for the True and the consequent for the False. Accordingly, our sentence is true if the Sun has not yet risen, whether the sky is very cloudy or not, and also if the Sun has risen and the sky is very cloudy. Since only truth-values are here in question, each component clause can be replaced by another of the same truth-value without changing the truth-value of the whole. (CP, p. 173.)

The sense of the sentence is equivalent to 'Either the Sun has not risen yet or the sky is very cloudy'. In accordance with all this, 'If the Sun has already risen, 5 is a prime number' will come out true if uttered before sunrise on a cloudy day. Frege is happy to accept this; the sentence, he agrees, will appear in a strange light, 'as if a sad melody were to be sung in a lively fashion' – but this is nothing to do with the truth-value. He suggests also that 'although' and 'but' can be treated as truth-functional, no less than 'and' and 'or' can.

Partly as a result of the work of Frege, philosophers now tend to think of propositions joined by truth-functional connectives as coordinated to each other on an equal level. Frege, however, was writing at a time when it was more natural to think of one of the component propositions as in some sense subordinate to the other. He says that whenever the reference of a subordinate clause is a truth-value, then it may be replaced, without harm to the truth-value of the whole, by a sentence having the same truth-value.

However, Frege recognizes that in the case of many kinds of subordinate clause this is simply not the case, and most of the concluding part of 'Sense and Reference' is devoted to showing that in such cases, contrary to the general rules, the reference of the clause is not a truth-value. He recognizes three main categories: direct quotation, indirect quotation and definite descriptions.

(1) If a sentence occurs within quotation marks, then the reference of the sentence is not a truth-value, but the words quoted, as in 'Smith said "The world will end in the year

2000"'. In such a case, Frege says, 'One's own words first designate words of the other speaker, and only the latter have their usual reference' (CP, p. 159).

(2) If a sentence occurs in reported speech, as in 'Smith said that the world will end in the year 2000', then the reference of the sentence, according to Frege, is what would normally be its sense. This, he says, is indirect reference as opposed to customary reference; and we can say that the indirect reference of a word is its customary sense (CP, pp. 159, 165). Does this mean that in this case the distinction between sense and reference collapses? No: Frege says that the clause has as sense (indirect sense, presumably) 'not a thought, but the sense of the words 'the thought, that . . .' which is only a part of the thought in the entire complex sentence' (CP, p. 166). Reports of thoughts, beliefs and inferences, and also hopes, regrets and similar feelings, are in this respect similar to indirect quotations: in all such cases the 'that' clauses refer to their sense and not to a truth-value (CP, p. 167).

It is easy to show that in such cases the clause does not occur truth-functionally. 'Copernicus believed that the planetary orbits are circular' and 'Copernicus believed that the Earth goes round the Sun' are both true, though the content of the first 'that' clause is false, and that of the second is true; and on the other hand, though the proposition 'Uranus goes round the Sun' is true no less than the proposition 'Venus goes round the Sun', the proposition 'Copernicus believed that Venus goes round the Sun' is true, while the proposition 'Copernicus believed that Uranus goes round the Sun' is false, since Uranus had not been discovered in Copernicus's day. Frege sums up

The main clause and the subordinate clause together have as their sense only a single thought, and the truth of the whole includes neither the truth nor the untruth of the subordinate clause. In such cases it is not permissible to replace one expression in the subordinate clause by another having the same customary reference, but only by one having the same indirect reference, i.e. the same customary sense. (CP, p. 166.)

This exception applies not only to the complete clauses, but also to names within them. In the sentence 'Duncan believed that Macbeth was trustworthy' we cannot substitute 'his murderer' for 'Macbeth'. The reference of the two expressions is the same, since Macbeth was Duncan's murderer, but Duncan never had the thought 'my murderer is trustworthy'.

Frege assimilates to the case of reported speech and belief a number of other constructions: indirect reports of commands and questions, and final clauses expressing a purpose. Consider the two sentences 'Napoleon believed that his right flank was to advance' and 'Napoleon gave orders that his right flank was to advance'. It is clear that a similar structure of argument and function can be discerned in the clause of the second sentence 'that his right flank was to advance' as in the clause of the first sentence 'that his right flank was to advance'. There is clearly something in common between the senses of the two clauses. The difference between the two is that if the two sentences were rewritten in direct speech, the first would contain a quotation in the assertoric mood, and the second would contain a quotation in the imperative mood. Frege sums this up by saying 'A command, a request, are indeed not thoughts, yet they stand on the same level as thoughts.' In subordinate clauses reporting commands, he says, words have their indirect reference.[3] In these clauses, as in those reporting statements and beliefs, the reference is not a truth-value; it is, he says, a command or request. From which we conclude that for Frege a command is the sense of an imperative sentence.

Frege deals very briefly with final clauses. 'Obviously', he says, 'a purpose is a thought; therefore: indirect reference for the words, subjunctive mood.' This seems questionable: Napoleon's purposes were surely what he wanted to bring about in the world, and it was not thoughts that he wanted to bring about. 'Napoleon took the necessary steps in order that his right flank should advance' seems to be closer to 'Napoleon gave orders

3. It is not clear to me what Frege would count as the direct reference of a sentence in the imperative.

that his right flank was to advance' than to 'Napoleon believed that his right flank was to advance', and so, even if one accepts Frege's case for the reference being indirect, it would seem that he should say that it is not to a thought, but to something analogous to a command or request.

Given Frege's account of reference, it is clear that in the cases where the reference of a clause is not a truth-value but a thought, a command or a purpose, the clause can be regarded as a proper name of the respective thought, command or purpose.

(3) Frege turns to a quite different group of cases, which would now be called (after Bertrand Russell) sentences containing definite descriptions. Consider the following sentence, adapted from Frege's own.

The man who discovered oxygen was guillotined.

Russell called expressions such as 'the man who discovered oxygen' definite descriptions, and he gave an elaborate analysis of the sentence in formal symbolism which was roughly equivalent in everyday language to the sentence 'one and only one man discovered oxygen, and that man was guillotined'.

Frege takes a different approach. He asks how we are to construe the relative clause

'who discovered oxygen'.

He says that such a clause does not have a thought occurring as its sense and a truth-value as its reference. It is not a complete thought; the grammatical subject 'who' has no independent sense and serves only to mediate a relationship with the main clause. The reference of the definite description is not a truth-value but an object, namely, the chemist Lavoisier.

One might think that the sense of the original sentence does include a thought as its part, namely, the thought that there was somebody who was the first to discover oxygen. At all events, nobody could take the sentence to be true who denied the existence of such a person. If 'the man who discovered oxygen' had no reference, the sentence could not be true.

Frege accepts this: but he says that the sentence does not state, but only presupposes, that there was somebody who was the first to discover oxygen. The sentence certainly presupposes that there was such a person, but that is quite different from containing, as part of the thought that it expresses, the thought that there was such a person. 'Lavoiser discovered oxygen' likewise presupposes that the name 'Lavoisier' has a reference; but that is not part of the thought that it expresses. If it were, the negation of 'Lavoisier was guillotined' would not be 'Lavoisier was not guillotined' but

> Either Lavoisier was not guillotined, or 'Lavoisier' has
> no reference.

That 'Lavoisier' has a reference is presupposed equally both by 'Lavoiser was guillotined' and by 'Lavoisier was not guillotined'. This shows the difference between the case where one sentence presupposes the truth of another and the case where one sentence has another as part of its sense.

So 'the man who discovered oxygen was guillotined' does not state, but only presupposes, that there was one and only one man who discovered oxygen. The interpretation of sentences of this kind which is here scorned by Frege was later explored, in a fertile manner, by Russell and his followers. But to this day there are philosophers who think that Frege's approach was the more appropriate one.

Frege believed that the possibility of a definite description lacking reference was to be averted not by particular provisions in individual sentences, but rather by general rules about the construction of scientific languages.

A logically perfect concept-script should satisfy the conditions, that every expression grammatically well constructed as a proper name out of signs already introduced shall in fact designate an object, and that no new sign shall be introduced as a proper name without being secured a reference. (CP, p. 169.)

What Frege has in mind here is illustrated by the example he gave in 'Function and Concept', where he says that we must see to it that we never perform calculations with empty signs in the belief that we are dealing with objects.

It is thus necessary to lay down rules from which it follows, e.g. what '⊙ + 1' is to stand for, if '⊙' is to stand for the Sun. What rule we lay down is a matter of comparative indifference; but it is essential that we should do so. (CP, p. 148.)

CHAPTER 8

GRUNDGESETZE DER ARITHMETIK, I

Grundgesetze der Arithmetik (The Basic Laws of Arithmetic) was intended by Frege to be the major work of his life, setting forth rigorously and completely his systematic derivation of arithmetic from logic. The first volume was published, with high hopes, in 1893, but by the time the second volume appeared in 1903 it had become clear that the programme could not be carried out in the way he had hoped. In this chapter I will describe the way in which the first volume develops (in a notation based on the *Concept Script*) the ideas presented, in a less formal manner, in *The Foundations of Arithmetic*.

The book begins with a long introduction. Frege explains that the proofs to be presented in the book are carried out entirely in symbols, in sequences of formulae each of which is a complete proposition. 'This completeness, not permitting the tacit attachment of presuppositions in thought, seems to me indispensable for the rigour of the conduct of proof.' Advance from one proposition to the next is permitted only in accordance with explicitly specified rules; all methods of inference must be specified in advance. Moreover, any definitions offered must make no pretence at being creative: they must be no more than abbreviations for complex terms, introduced to simplify the setting out of proofs.

Frege explains his method as a development of the Euclidean method. We cannot demand that everything be proved, because that is impossible; but we can require that all propositions used without proof be expressly declared as such, and we can reduce to the minimum the number of these primitive propositions.

Frege calls his unproved propositions or axioms 'basic laws', which gives its title to the book.

Some mathematicians claim that arithmetic is a more highly developed logic. If this claim is to be more than vague hand-waving, it can only be established if proofs of arithmetical propositions are laid out in logically simple steps which leave no room for any tacit appeal to intuition. If this is done – and this was Frege's intention – any error in the system can be clearly located, either in the axioms, or the definitions, or in the rules or their application. With remarkable prescience Frege announces that the only possible place where a question might be raised is in connection with the fifth of the axioms of his system, an axiom which introduces the value-ranges which, in 'Function and Concept', he added to the system of *Concept Script*. We shall discuss this axiom later, and we shall see that his unease over this point proved to be justified.

In the introduction, Frege goes out of his way to prepare his readers for the extraordinary length of the proofs which he is about to offer for obvious truths of arithmetic. The length of a proof, he says, is not to be measured by the yard: proofs can be made to look short by skipping steps. The ordinary mathematical reader will, quite reasonably, be content if each step is evidently correct; but if we wish to gain an insight into what exactly it is for a mathematical truth to be evident, then all the intermediate steps have to be laid out for examination.

Frege emphasizes that the view of number he now presents in 1893 is the same as the one in the *Foundations* in 1884. The fundamental principle remains that a statement of number expresses an assertion about a concept. Statements of numbers are concerned with sets of aggregates only in so far as these are classes determined by a concept, that is, by the properties an object must have in order to belong to the class.

The project to be presented was already in view at the time of the *Concept Script* in 1879, and the notation to be used is basically the same. Frege draws attention, however, to a number of developments in the system. (1) The symbol '$\equiv$' used in

Concept Script for identity of content has now been replaced by the ordinary identity sign. (2) A notation is introduced for value-ranges, following the introduction of this notion in 'Function and Concept' (CP, p. 143). (3) A quite new sign is introduced, which is to do the work done by the definite article in ordinary language.

In connection with value-ranges Frege says:

Value-ranges are extremely important in principle; in fact I define number itself as the extension of a concept, and extensions of concepts are by my definitions value-ranges. Thus we just cannot get on without them. (BLA, p. 6.)

In addition to these symbolic innovations, Frege draws attention to two changes in the philosophical interpretation of the symbolism. First, the horizontal stroke is now taken in a different way, since 'content' has now been distinguished into sense and reference. Secondly, and consequently, the two truth-values, the True and the False, have been identified as the reference of sentences.

Frege addresses himself in this book to both mathematicians and philosophers, but without great hope of being fully understood by either. Many mathematicians, he complains, when they meet expressions like 'concept' and 'relation' are turned off by what they see as metaphysical, and many philosophers, when they see symbols on the page, skip to the next non-mathematical passage. Also few mathematicians take a serious interest in the foundations of mathematics; and those that do are all too likely to adopt a formalist standpoint, and claim that mathematics is simply a game like chess.

Here Frege repeats his familiar attack on the formalist notion of creative definition.

One cannot by pure definition magically conjure into a thing a property that in fact it does not possess – save that of now being called by the name with which one has named it. That an oval figure produced on paper with ink should by a definition acquire the property of yielding one when added to one, I can only regard as a scientific superstition.

One could just as well by a pure definition make a lazy pupil diligent. (BLA, p. 11.)

Frege says that if contemporary mathematicians are all formalists, contemporary logicians are all psychologistic. They produce thick textbooks, bloated with unhealthy psychological fat that conceals all more delicate forms (BLA, p. 24). Logicians consider, instead of things themselves, only images, subjective simulacra. They confuse the normative laws of logic with the descriptive laws of psychology. If the laws of thought are psychological they will, no doubt, tell one how the average person thinks. If one wishes to be an average person, then one might use these principles to tell one how to conform to the average. They would be like principles telling one how to speak grammatically or to dress fashionably.

But just as what is fashionable in dress at the moment will shortly be fashionable no longer and among the Chinese is not fashionable now, so these psychological laws of thought can be laid down only with restrictions on their authority. (BLA, p. 13.)

Psychologistic logicians confuse something's being true with its being taken to be true. But the two are quite different; there is no contradiction in a thing's being true while everybody takes it to be false.

If it is true that I am writing this in my chamber on the 13th of July 1893, while the wind howls out of doors, then it remains true even if all men should subsequently take it to be false. (BLA, p. 13.)

The laws of logic are not psychological laws: they are eternal boundary stones which our thought can overflow but never displace. The law of identity, for instance, is to be stated

> Every object is identical with itself

and not

> It is impossible for people in the year 1893 to acknowledge an object as being different from itself.

Psychologism, according to Frege, leads to idealism and eventually to solipsism.

If every man designated something different by the name 'moon', namely one of his own images, much as he expresses his own pain by the cry 'ouch', then of course the psychological point of view would be justified; but an argument about the properties of the moon would be pointless: one person could perfectly well assert of his moon the opposite of what the other person, with equal right, said of his ... There would be no logic to be appointed arbiter in the conflict of opinions. (BLA, p. 23.)

If we want to emerge from this subjectivity, we have to accept that our knowledge does not create what is known but grasps what is already there. When I grasp a pencil, many physiological changes take place in my body, but they neither are the pencil nor create the pencil; similarly, when I grasp something with my mind, many psychological phenomena may accompany or be involved in this grasping, but what is grasped is neither identical with nor created by these events in my mental life.

The opening section of the *Grundgesetze*, section 0 of the book, contains only two items which add to what we already know. First, Frege makes clear the nature of his objection to the notion of 'set'. What is wrong is to regard a set as being defined by enumeration of its elements. He is willing to accept the notion of set provided that it is equivalent to what Boole called a 'class' and what Dedekind called a 'system'. According to Dedekind

A system S ... is completely determined if for every thing it is determined whether it is an element of S or not. Hence a system S is the same as a system T (in symbols, $S = T$) if every element of S is also an element of T and every element of T is also an element of S. (BLA, p. 30.)

Frege is willing to allow this as an acceptable notion of set or class. We determine a class by specifying a concept (perhaps by listing its component characteristics) and then defining the class as the class of objects falling under that concept. With this definition there is no difficulty about the notion of an empty class: it is the set defined by any concept under which no objects fall. On the other hand, the empty class is an absurdity if sets are to be given by listing their elements.

Secondly, Frege makes an explicit commitment to a strict, even pedantic, use of quotation marks, 'By their use', he says, 'I distinguish between the cases where I am speaking of the sign itself, and those where I am speaking about what it stands for.' In his own earlier writings, Frege had not always been punctilious about this. Even now, he does not make explicit a further convention which he adopts (and has employed since 'Function and Concept') whereby italics are employed to speak about a (non-linguistic) function. Italics are also used in *Grundgesetze*, as elsewhere, for emphasis, or to introduce newly defined terms. It is only in rare cases that this leads to confusion, but it shows that there was still a long way to go if Frege was to achieve his own ideal of the rigorous exclusion of signifier-signified ambiguity.

The notion of function is introduced in section 1 of the *Grundgesetze*. In general, it is presented in the same way as in 'Function and Concept'. Here, as there, Frege rejects the idea that a function is a certain kind of expression, and goes on to reject, as a second false start, the idea that a function is what a certain kind of expression stands for. The essence of a function (such as $(2 - x) + x^2$) appears only when we substitute numerals for 'x'. The essence of the function shows itself in the connection established between the numbers whose signs we put in place of 'x' and the numbers that appear as the references of the expressions which we form by our substitutions.[1] Frege says:

The expression for a *function* is *in need of completion, unsaturated*. The letter 'x' serves only to hold places open for a numeral that is to

---

1. Such a connection, Frege says, is 'intuitively represented in the course of the curve whose equation in rectangular coordinates is "$y = (2 + 3x^2)x$"'. Earlier, in 'Function and Concept', it was not the function itself, but its value-range which was compared to the curve.

complete the expression, and in this way renders recognizable the particular type of need for completion that constitutes the specific nature of the function symbolized above. (BLA, p. 34.)

Frege introduces the notions of *argument* and *value* as in his earlier works, and then continues

We obtain a name of the value of a function for an argument, if we fill the argument places in the name of the function with the name of the argument.

Thus, for instance, '$(2 - 1) + 1$' is a name of the number 2, composed of the numeral '1' and the name of the function mentioned above.

In the first passage it is clear that a function-expression, no less than a function itself, is something incomplete and unsaturated. This fits well with the description of linguistic functions given in the *Concept Script*, though Frege now partially disowns the account of functions given in that work, since it failed to make a clear distinction between linguistic functions and the functions they express. It comes as a surprise that Frege, having recognized that a symbol for a function must itself share the function's incompleteness, should go on in the second passage quoted above to speak of 'function-names', since a name, according to the theory he has propounded hitherto, is a complete and saturated sign. Henceforth Frege extends the use of 'name' to include linguistic functions, and uses 'proper name' where hitherto he has used 'name'. For instance, a few pages later he says

The names of objects – or proper names – carry no argument-places; they are saturated, like the objects themselves. (BLA, p. 36.)

Whereas hitherto he spoke of 'names' and 'predicates' he is now preferring to speak of 'proper names' and 'function-names'. The earlier terminology was surely preferable.[2]

---

2. What Frege calls a 'function-name' is not an actual expression occurring in his symbolism but a pattern discernible when the name of a value is formed from the name of an argument.

Frege's expansion of the mathematical notion of function, and the extension of possible arguments to all objects including truth-values, is set out in sections two and four of *Grundgesetze*. These passages merely abbreviate, and add nothing to, the corresponding passages in 'Function and Concept' (see pp. 107–8 above). In section three of *Grundgesetze*, however, there is a striking difference between the way in which value-ranges are introduced and the way in which they made their appearance in 'Function and Concept'.

Frege begins, now as then, by saying that two functions have the same value-ranges if and only if they always have the same value for the same argument. But whereas in 'Function and Concept' he goes on immediately to introduce a special symbolism for value-ranges, in *Grundgesetze* he says that, given appropriate definitions, the function

$$(\xi^2 = 4) = (3\xi^2 = 12)$$

always has the True as its value.

Since, here as in 'Function and Concept', a function whose value is always a truth-value is a concept, we can call the value-range of such a function the extension of the concept. Hence, Frege can say that the formula above is equivalent to 'the concept *square root of 4* has the same extension as the concept *something whose square trebled is 12*' (BLA, p. 36).

Frege introduces functions of two arguments at this point. These, he says, are doubly in need of completion. When one of its argument places is filled, we are left with a function of one argument. For instance, $\xi(\xi + 2\zeta)$ is a function of the two arguments ξ and ζ; by substituting '1' for 'ζ' we partially saturate that function. In its place we have the function $\xi(\xi + 2)$, which is a function of one argument. If we saturate this in turn by substituting '3' for 'ξ', we obtain the value 15. 'Only by means of a second completion', Frege says, 'do we arrive at an object, and this is then called the value of the function for the two arguments.' (BLA, p. 36.)

Some two-argument functions will have, for any pair of

arguments, a truth-value for their value. Such will be, given appropriate definitions, the functions $\xi = \zeta$, and ξ *is greater than* ζ. Just as Frege defined a concept as being a one-argument function whose value is always a truth-value, so now he defines a relation as being a two-argument function whose value is always a truth-value. If $\Phi(A, B)$ holds, then A stands in the relation $\Phi(\xi, \zeta)$ to B.

In section 5 Frege introduces his judgement stroke, distinguishing between truth and assertion in his usual manner: '2 + 3 = 5' merely denotes the True; only if the special sign for assertion is added does it *say that* it is true. The horizontal line which in the *Concept Script* was called the 'content-stroke' is now called simply 'the horizontal', since the notion of *content* is now regarded, since the distinction between sense and reference was introduced, as involving a confusion of thought and truth-value.

The horizontal stroke is itself a functional sign. So, ——A is the True if A is the True; otherwise it is the False. This definition means that ——A is the False not only if A is the False, but also if A is not a truth-value at all. Thus the value of ——5 is the False. This stipulation is an instance of Frege's carrying out, in his definitions, the requirement that no names without reference may be allowed in a scientific language such as his concept-script. Moreover since ——ξ is a function whose value is always a truth-value, ——ξ is, by Frege's definition, a concept. It is a concept under which only the True falls.

Frege next introduces a negation-sign '—┬', laying down that the value of ┬ξ is to be the False for every argument for which the value of ——ξ is the True, and to be the True for all other arguments.[3] Thus '┬(5 = 4)' is equivalent to the sentence of ordinary language '5 is not 4'. It follows from Frege's definition, as we should expect, that negation of a proposition is a truth-function of that proposition, that is to say, that the truth-value

3. In explaining the notation of *Concept Script* I used a modern notation for negation. Here I use Frege's own sign, to bring out the relationship between negation and the content-stroke and the way in which in the new system negation can be applied to items other than propositions. In the modern notation, '——┐5' would simply be ill-formed.

of the negation depends on the truth-value of what is negated. But that is not all that follows from Frege's definition. If what is negated is not a proposition at all, then the negation, on his stipulation, comes out true. So '⌐5' on his definition names the True no less than '⌐(5 = 4)'. Frege says that negation is a concept under which falls every object except the True.

The symbolism for generality, and the notion of scope, are introduced in the *Grundgesetze* in essentially the same way as in the *Concept Script*. The differences in exposition arise only from two causes: first, Frege's new policy of treating sentences as names of truth-values, and, secondly, his increased scrupulousness in adding stipulations to ensure that no sign or well-formed combination of signs shall lack a reference.

It is in sections 9 and 10 that the *Grundgesetze* marks a significant development beyond that of *Concept Script*, namely in the exposition of the symbolism for value-ranges, first introduced in 'Function and Concept'. If two functions, Φ and Ψ, have the same value for every argument (so that $(x)\ \Phi x = \Psi x$), then, as has already been stipulated, the two functions have the same value-range. We can transform a generalized identity into the identity of a value-range.

The possibility must be regarded as a law of logic, a law that is invariably employed, even if tacitly, whenever discussion is carried on about the extensions of concepts. (BLA, p. 44.)

Frege recalls that in *The Foundations of Arithmetic* he had defined a number as the extension of a concept. He now gives a reason why it is essential to make the step from generalized identities to identity of value-range. Because a value-range is an object, we can set down a simple sign for a value-range and thus introduce a proper name for a number. However, in

$$(x)\ (\Phi(x) = \Psi(x))'$$

we cannot put a single symbol for '$\Phi(x)$', because the letter 'x' must always occur in whatever is substituted for '$\Phi(x)$'.

To construct symbols for value-ranges, Frege introduces, as he did in 'Function and Concept', the symbol consisting of a Greek letter capped with the sign ' (the smooth breathing). So $\acute{\varepsilon}(\varepsilon^2 = 4)$ is the value range of the function $\xi^2 = 4$, or the extension of the concept *square root of 4*, and in general '$\acute{\varepsilon}\Phi(\varepsilon)$' denotes the value-range of the function $\Phi(\xi)$. 'The introduction of a notation for value-ranges', Frege says, 'seems to me to be one of the most important additions I have made to my concept script since my first publication on the subject.' (BLA, p. 45).

When this notation was first introduced by Frege in 'Function and Concept', value-ranges were, as we saw, explained as being comparable to curves on a graph. That made it natural to understand them as a set of ordered pairs of arguments and values. But now in *Grundgesetze* Frege seems, in the application which he makes of the symbolism, to be much closer to regarding the value-range of a concept as being the class of objects that fall under it.

Frege's current understanding of value-ranges is made clearest in a footnote to p. 48 of BLA. There Frege considers the suggestion that every object might be regarded as a value-range, namely as the extension of a concept under which it and it alone falls. A concept under which an object A and A alone falls is the concept $\xi = A$. So we might be tempted, Frege says, to make the stipulation that $\acute{\varepsilon}(\varepsilon = A)$ is to be the same as A. He at once goes on to reject the suggestion; but not on the grounds that an object such as, say, Julius Caesar is very different from a set of ordered pairs of the kind {Julius Caesar, The True; Augustus, The False etc.}.[4]

The notion of value-range is to put to use in Frege's second innovation, made for the first time in *Grundgesetze*. This is the introduction of a function which is to have a role in the concept

---

4. The clearest explanation given by Frege of his understanding at this time of the relationship between predicates and their senses and references, and concepts

script similar to that of the definite article when it occurs in expressions such as 'The negative square root of four'.

Suppose that we consider an example used in an earlier chapter (see p. 139 above),

> The man who discovered oxygen was guillotined.

We saw that Frege agreed that this sentence could not be true unless one and only one man discovered oxygen, but he denied that this was something asserted by anyone who asserted the sentence; it was, rather, presupposed. Now if one and only one man discovered oxygen, then only one object falls under the concept ξ *discovered oxygen*. We know, in fact, that this object is Lavoisier. Hence, the value of ξ *discovered oxygen* for any argument is the same as the value of $\xi = Lavoisier$ for any argument. By Frege's definition, therefore, the value-ranges of the two functions are the same:

$$\dot{\varepsilon}(\varepsilon \text{ discovered oxygen}) = \dot{\alpha}(\alpha = \text{Lavoisier}).$$

And in general, if one and only one object A falls under a concept Φ, the value-range $\dot{\varepsilon}\Phi(\varepsilon)$ is the same as the value range $\dot{\alpha}(\alpha = A)$.

---

and their extensions, comes not in the *Grundgesetze* itself but in a letter to Husserl of 1891. He sets out the following schema:

Sentence	Proper name	Concept word	
Sense of sentence	Sense of proper name	Sense of word	
Reference of sentence (Truth-value)	Reference of proper name (Object)	Reference of concept word → (Concept)	Object which falls under concept

He goes on to say, 'in the case of the concept-word there is one step more to get to the object than there is in the case of a proper name; and the object may be missing – that is, the concept can be empty – without thereby the concept's ceasing to be scientifically useful. I have written the last step from the concept to the object sideways to indicate that it is on the same level, that objects and concepts have the same objectivity.' (See FA, p. 47; PMC, p. 96.)

Frege makes use of this to introduce a function $/\xi$, which is intended to correspond to the definite article in definite descriptions. The definition of this function involves two stipulations, of which the first is as follows. Wherever the argument ξ is a value-range identical with a value-range $\dot{\alpha}(\alpha = A)$ corresponding to an object A, then the value of the function is A itself. It follows from this that the value of $/\dot{\alpha}(\alpha = \textit{Lavoisier})$ is Lavoisier, and so is the value of $/\dot{\epsilon}(\epsilon \textit{ discovered oxygen})$, since these value-ranges are identical. Hence we can use the expression '$/\dot{\epsilon}(\epsilon$ discovered oxygen)' as equivalent to 'the discoverer of oxygen', and in general '$/\dot{\epsilon}\Phi(\epsilon)$ can be substituted for 'the Φ-er'.

But the stipulation just made about the value of $/\xi$ is insufficient to define it, if it is to meet Frege's requirement that the value of every function be defined for every possible argument. For suppose that there is not just one object which falls under the concept Φ; suppose, for instance, that 'the Φ-er' is 'the discoverer of the differential calculus'. Since both Newton and Leibniz made this discovery independently the value-range $\dot{\epsilon}(\epsilon$ discovered the calculus) is not identical either with $\dot{\alpha}(\alpha = $ Newton) or with $\dot{\alpha}(\alpha = $ Leibniz). There is, indeed, no value range of the form $\dot{\alpha}(\alpha = A)$ identical with the value-range of the concept ξ *discovered the calculus*. For such cases, Frege adds a second limb to his definition of the function $/\xi$. Whenever the argument of the function does not satisfy the condition laid down in the first limb, then the value of the function is to be the argument itself. Thus, for instance, the value of $/\dot{\epsilon}(\epsilon^2 = 1)$ is just $\dot{\epsilon}(\epsilon^2 = 1)$, because there is more than one square root of 1 (BLA, p. 50).

Frege says that his stipulation ensures that '$/\dot{\epsilon}\Phi(\epsilon)$' always has a reference, whether the function $\Phi(x)$ is or is not a concept, and whether it is a concept under which there falls no object, or more than one, or exactly one object. Presumably, if the argument of $/\xi$ is not a value-range at all, but some other kind of object, it is equally assured of a sense under the second limb of the definition: thus the value of $/\textit{Julius Caesar}$ will be none other than Julius Caesar himself.

In section 12 of the *Grundgesetze* Frege introduces the definitions of the truth-functional connectives. First, he defines the symbol corresponding to the truth-functional conditional 'If p then q' (understood as meaning that either p is false or q is true), next that corresponding to 'and' ('p and q' being defined, in effect, as 'It is not the case that if p then not q') and finally 'neither–nor' and the inclusive 'or'.[5] These symbols are introduced in essentially the same manner was was explained confusedly in the *Concept Script* and clearly in 'Function and Concept'. But it is to be noted that according to Frege's new passion for treating almost all symbols as names, the '→' symbol itself has the role of a name, a name of the two-argument function $\xi \to \zeta$.

Frege observes that in his symbolism the sentential-connective 'and' appears to be less simple than the truth-functional conditional sign, for which a simple expression in words is lacking, 'if ... then' being appropriate only in certain contexts. He says that the relation in ordinary language seems more natural because we are used to it. From a logical standpoint, it is hard to say which is simpler; the truth-functional conditional can be defined in terms of conjunction and negation, but, equally, conjunction can be defined in terms of the truth-functional conditional and negation. The reason Frege gives for taking the truth-functional conditional as primitive is the ease by which it can be used to present deductive inference.

Frege accordingly proceeds to set out his methods of inference. The first is his version of *modus ponens*: From A and $A \to B$ infer B. This, Frege says, is the only method of inference used in the original *Concept Script* and one can manage with it alone; but to shorten lengthy chains of inference, it is necessary to introduce additional rules. The particular rules introduced by Frege now have only historical interest, and it is unnecessary to specify them here.

5. Frege uses not the propositional variables 'p', 'q', 'r' but the Greek capital letters which he uses as variables for names of objects. This is in accordance with the thesis that sentences are names of truth-values.

The next section of the *Grundgesetze* to raise questions of abiding philosophical interest is section 21, where Frege introduces his distinction between first- and second-level functions. We saw in *Concept Script* that '$\neg (x) \neg (x^2 = 4)$' and '$\neg (x) \neg (x$ is greater than 0)' can both be regarded as instances of a more general expression '$\neg (x) \neg \Phi(x)$, obtained by replacing the function expression '$\Phi(\ldots)$' by the function-expressions '$\ldots^2 = 4$' and '$\ldots$ is greater than 0'. Now suppose we have a function where the argument sign in '$X(\xi)$' is replaced by '$\Phi(\xi)$'. Frege says:

We commonly speak here of a 'function of a function', but inaccurately; for if we recall that functions are fundamentally different from objects, and further that the value of a function for an argument is to be distinguished from the function itself, then we see that a function-name can never occupy the place of a proper name, because it carries with it empty places that answer to the unsaturatedness of the function. If we say 'the function $\Phi(\xi)$', then we must never forget that 'ξ' belongs to the function-name only in the sense that it renders this unsaturatedness recognizable. Thus another function can never occur as argument of the function $X(\xi)$, though indeed the value of a function for an argument can do so: e.g. $\Phi(2)$, in which case the value is $X(\Phi 2)$). (BLA, p. 73.)

The function-name does not really appear, in such a case, as an argument of $X(\xi)$, because the function-name fills up only a part of the argument place.

However, in '$\neg (x) \neg \Phi(x)$' we have an expression in which we can replace the functional expression '$\Phi(\xi)$' by expressions for functions of one argument, but not by names of objects, and not by names of functions of more than one argument. So '$\neg (x) \neg (x^2 = 4)$', '$\neg (x) \neg (x$ is greater than 0)' can both be regarded as values of the same function for different arguments, but where the arguments are themselves functions, they can be regarded as functions of a single argument. A function of this kind is clearly different from a function whose arguments are objects.

We now call those functions whose arguments are objects *first-level functions*; on the other hand, those functions whose arguments are first-level functions may be called *second-level functions*. (BLA, p. 74.)

A second-level function whose value is always a truth-value may be called a second-level concept.

Frege gives, in section 22, examples of second-level functions. One such is $\Phi(2)$. Some of the values of this function are numbers; for instance, for the argument $\xi + 1$ the value of this function is 3. Others are truth-values; for instance, for the argument $\xi + 1 = 4$ the value is the False. 'This second-level function', Frege says, 'is distinct from the number 2 itself, since, like all functions, it is unsaturated.' (BLA, p. 75.)

Frege uses his horizontal stroke to construct a function $——\Phi(2)$ which marks out those functions of 2 whose value is always a truth-value. This function is therefore a second-level concept which, he says, we may call 'property of the number 2'. All and only those first-level concepts under which 2 falls, fall under this second-level concept.

In addition to first-level and second-level functions there are also unequal-levelled concepts. One example is the first derivative of a function in analysis, which is a function of two arguments, the first of which must be a first-level function, and the second an object.

We also have an unequal-levelled function of two arguments in $——\Phi(\xi)$, where 'ξ' occupies and renders recognizable the place of the object-argument, and '$\Phi(\ )$' that of the function-argument. Since the value of this function is always a truth-value, we can call it an unequal-levelled relation. It is the relation of an object to a concept under which it falls. (BLA, p. 76.)

An example of a second-level concept whose argument must be a function of two arguments is the many–oneness of a relation. This is defined, following the lines of *The Foundations of Arithmetic*, as follows: If $X(\xi, \zeta)$ is a relation such that from

$X(a, b)$ and $X(a, c)$ it follows universally that $c = b$, then $X(\xi, \zeta)$ is a many–one relation.

How are we to express generality with respect to second-level functions? Here again we have an innovation in the *Grundgesetze*. Let us start by considering second-level functions of one argument (such as *being a property of the number two* or *having an object falling under it*). Frege introduces the notation

$$M_\beta(\Phi(\beta))$$

as a variable which is to range over such second-level functions of one argument in the same way as $f(\xi)$ was to range over first-level functions of one argument. The capital italic letter M is a variable to indicate that we are talking of functions of a second level; the β which is a subscript to it is to show that it is to range over functions which can apply to functions with only one argument; and the '$\Phi(\beta)$' marks the argument place to be filled with the function replacing 'Φ' – the 'β' here indicates that the function in question must also be a function which takes a single argument. The variable which Frege introduces here is used only at one place in the development of his system, in a single axiom, which can be rendered in English thus:

Every second-level function which holds for all first-level single-argument functions holds for any first-level single-argument function. (BLA, p. 80.)

The formulation of this axiom involves making use of a *third-level* function holding for second-level functions, namely

$$(f)\, M_\beta(f(\beta)).$$

It would have been possible to introduce a variable $M_\beta d(\Phi(\beta, d))$ to range over second-level functions which can hold for functions of more than one argument (such as a relation's being many–one, or being symmetrical). Frege, however, does not do so (BLA, p. 87). Instead, he adopts what he calls a more economical way of expressing generality with respect to these functions, by taking the value-range of a function as a proxy for the function itself. Since a value-range is an object, we are always able to make use of functions whose arguments are objects, rather than higher-level functions whose arguments are lower-level functions.

CHAPTER 9

GRUNDGESETZE DER ARITHMETIK, II

Having in the first chapter of the *Grundgesetze* presented his primitive signs, Frege devotes the second chapter to the topic of definitions. Definition, he insists, is a process merely of abbreviation; and to express definition he introduces, as in *Concept Script*, the sign ⊩—. A definition is a stipulation that a newly introduced sign is to have the same sense and reference as a complex sign composed of familiar signs. Thus, in Frege's text, a definition will be of the following form:

> ⊩— definiens (old complex sign) = definiendum
> (new simpler sign).

Once the sign has been introduced, the definition becomes a truth and can itself be used as a proposition or theorem of the system.

After introducing the definition sign, Frege sets out rules of well-formedness for names in his formal system: they must be signs introduced either as primitive, or by definition, and they must obey the conventions laid down for the kind of name to which they belong. Every well-formed name must have a reference; and this is to be secured by a recursive procedure. We start from a set of primitive names and their references, and then set out rules for the extension, step by step, of the sphere of such names.

We must remember that by this point in Frege's development the sense of the word 'name' has become extremely wide. Proper names, which are names of objects, include entire sentences, which are names of truth-values; and, as well as proper names, there are names of functions.

In asking, for the purposes of his system, in what circumstances names have reference, Frege cannot make use of the examples from ordinary life and language which he employed in the informal exposition of his philosophy in *The Foundations of Arithmetic* and in papers like 'Function and Concept', because the existence of objects like Julius Caesar and the Moon is a matter of empirical fact. At the beginning of the formalization of logic, the only objects whose existence can be taken for granted are the two truth-values, the True and the False.

The primitive vocabulary of the *Grundgesetze* consists of eight symbols introduced in the previous chapter. None of them are names of objects; all of them are names of functions.

Three of these names are names of first-level functions of one argument:

$$\text{`---}\xi\text{'}, \qquad \text{`---}\xi\text{'}, \qquad \text{`}/\xi\text{'}.$$

Two are names of first-level functions of two arguments:

$$\text{`}\xi \rightarrow \zeta\text{'}, \qquad \text{`}x = z\text{'}.$$

Two are names of second-level functions of one argument:

$$\text{`}(x)\,\Phi(x)\text{'} \qquad \text{`}\grave{\varepsilon}\Phi(\varepsilon)\text{'}.$$

One is the name of a third-level function

$$(f)\,M_\beta(f(\beta)).$$

Frege starts from the fact that the names of truth-values stand for something, and then widens the sphere of names by showing how new names can be formed from old names by the insertion of an existing name into an appropriate argument place in another existing name. He lays down detailed stipulations for the recursive construction of names in this way, and shows how they are to be applied to the primitive names. We may give a single, comparatively simple, example to illustrate his procedure.

The name of a single-argument first-level function has a reference, he says, if the proper name which results from filling

161

its argument place with a name with a reference is itself a proper name with a reference. This is verified, for instance, in the case of the name of the negation function; if we put the name of a truth-value in the argument place of $\smile \xi$ the result is itself the name of a truth-value. This follows from the definition of negation.

The notion of a proper name seems intuitively simpler than that of a function name; and indeed it is used in spelling out the condition for a function name to have reference. The reason why Frege introduces this latter condition before he introduces the condition for a proper name to have reference is that at the beginning of the system of the *Grundgesetze* we have only function names, and the only objects to be named are the truth-values. The first proper names will be the axioms of the system, which are names of the True.

Frege shows, in rather painful detail, that each of the eight primitive names has a reference. He goes on to prove that the same holds good of all names compounded out of these in accordance with his rules. He tells us that all well-formed names possess not only a reference, but a sense.

Every such name of a truth-value expresses a sense, a thought. Namely, by our stipulations it is determined under what conditions the name denotes the True. The sense of this name – the *thought* – is the thought that these conditions are fulfilled. (BLA, p. 90.)

Not all names, of course, are names of truth-values, even at this primitive stage of the development of the *Grundgesetze*. The primitive signs, for instance, are names of functions. These signs too have senses, and Frege explains what their senses are in the following passage:

The names, whether simple or themselves composite, of which the name of a truth-value consists, contribute to the expression of the thought, and this contribution of the individual components is its *sense*. If a name is part of the name of a truth-value, then the sense of the former name is part of the thought expressed by the latter name. (BLA, p. 90.)

These two passages are of great philosophical importance. Here, in a single page of the *Grundgesetze*, we find enunciated two theses that were to prove extremely influential in later philosophy: that the sense of words is given by their contribution to the sense of the sentences in which they occur, and that the sense of these sentences themselves is given by the conditions under which they hold true.

Frege now proceeds to lay out seven principles for the introduction of definitions. The most important are the first four discussed below (the remaining three deal with details of notation).

1. Every name reached by definitions must have a reference, which will be guaranteed if it is translatable back into the eight primitive names.

2. The same sign may never be defined more than once, for fear of inconsistency between different definitions.

3. A new name to be introduced must be simple, and must not contain any terms introduced at a different time; again this is to rule out the possibility of inconsistency.

4. The left-hand side of the definitional identity (the definiens) must contain a name formed from primitive or already defined names, and the right-hand sign (the definiendum) must contain a simple sign not previously employed. The definition introduces the definiendum as a sign of equivalent meaning which may replace, or be replaced by, the definiens.

It is in the course of the second volume of *Grundgesetze* that Frege sets out in detail his philosophical views on the nature of definition (GB, pp. 159–72). Every sound definition, he lays down, must satisfy two principles: the principle of completeness and the principle of simplicity. The principle of simplicity requires that the symbol to be defined be simple; the principle of completeness requires that the definition itself be complete.

Frege says that to be complete the definition of a predicate must provide for its occurrence in every possible context. The concept expressed by a predicate must have a sharp boundary;

that is to say, it must be determined for every object whether or not it falls under the concept. If there were objects for which this was not so, then the concept would not have a sharp boundary, but would in places have fuzzy edges shading into the background. Similarly, a predicate which expresses a concept must be defined in such a way that it is determined, for every object, whether or not it is truly assertible of it.

What is meant by 'determined' here? Surely only an omniscient being could know of each and every predicate, in the case of each single object, whether or not it was true? What Frege means is that the definition of a predicate must lay down unambiguously the conditions under which it is true of an object. This will suffice for the predicate, and the underlying concept, to be determinate, even though there may be many cases where we ignorant humans may not be able to decide whether the conditions are or are not fulfilled.

A concept which is not completely defined, in this sense, is only a quasi-concept, just as a proper name with no reference is only a quasi-name. Quasi-concepts, Frege says, are unamenable to logic. Even the most basic laws of logic do not hold of them. Take the law of excluded middle: either $\Phi(X)$ or not $\Phi(X)$. If 'Φ' expresses nothing more than a quasi-concept, then there will be at least one object X for which neither '$\Phi(X)$' nor '$\!-\!\Phi(X)$' will hold. 'Has the question "Are we still Christians?" really got a sense, if it is indeterminate whom the predicate "Christian" can truly be asserted of, and who must be refused it?' (GB, p. 159).

If we require completeness in definitions of concepts we must make the same requirement for functions of all kinds. If the expression 'the half of . . .' were not defined for all arguments, then a concept such as that represented by the predicate '. . . is such that the half of it is less than one' would also be incomplete. So we must define 'the half of . . .' in such a way that the expression 'the half of the Moon' has a definite reference, which in ordinary language it lacks since it is quite indeterminate which part of the Moon is meant.

If the condition of completeness is accepted, very severe restraints are placed on the practice of mathematicians. It was common for mathematicians to first define a function for a limited domain of objects – for example, positive integers – and much later, after having long made use of the function, to define it afresh for a domain including different objects – for example, negative integers and zero.

Frege insists that piecemeal definition of this kind must be rejected. If the first definition of the function leaves it as an open question what values it takes for arguments from the wider domain, then it already violates the principle of completeness. If on the other hand the first definition is complete from the outset and has drawn sharp boundaries to the function, we may ask whether the second definition draws the same boundaries as the first, or if it draws different ones. In the first case, the coincidence of the boundaries is something which needs proof and cannot be laid down, and we should avoid definitions which presuppose the carrying out of a proof. In the second case the difference between the boundaries means that the two definitions contradict each other.

Piecemeal definition also undermines the theorems which have already been proved. For instance, if the words 'square root of 9' have been defined with a restriction to the domain of positive integers, then we can prove that there is only one square root of nine. But this theorem is overthrown once the definition is extended to negative numbers and we have -3 and 3 as the square roots of 9. And how do we know that there are only two such square roots? May not some later definition oblige us to recognize four or eight? 'If we have no final definitions we likewise have no final theorems. We never emerge from incompleteness and vagueness.' (GB, p. 165.)

What applies to concepts (one-place functions whose values are always truth-values) must also apply to relations (two-place functions whose values are always truth-values). If a relation like *greater than* were not completely defined, then a concept like *greater than zero* would likewise lack complete definition.

Yet mathematicians, Frege complains, are happy to offer piece-meal definitions not only of predicates like '. . . is greater than' but even of the ' = ' sign itself.

The requirement to define mathematical functions and concepts for objects of all kinds is an irksome one, and it might be thought that we could render it unnecessary by stipulating that the expressions for such functions are to have a reference only when the arguments are numbers. Consider the concept *something that gives the result one when added to itself*, which is expressed by the predicate '$\xi + \xi = 1$'.

Under the suggested stipulation we will know that 'the Moon + the Moon = 1' is not true, since the Moon is not a number. But this will not suffice to make the plus sign well defined. For by our stipulation 'the Moon + the Moon' will not have a reference, and hence the sentence 'It is not the case that the Moon + the Moon = 1' will not be true either, and there will once again be a violation of the principle of the excluded middle.

There is another way by which we might try to avoid the requirement of complete definition. We might take care, when stating laws containing expressions defined only for numbers, to make the restriction to numbers a condition of the law itself. Thus:

If a is a number and b is a number then $a + b = b + a$.

But the following proposition can, after some manipulation, be proved from this proposition:

If $\neg (a + b = b + a)$ and a is a number then b is not a number.

This second proposition cannot be put forward if the domain is restricted to numbers. But if the domain is not so restricted, then the antecedent clause only has a sense if the plus sign has been completely defined.

Accordingly, Frege concludes, conditional definition, like piecemeal definition, must be rejected. 'Every symbol must be completely defined at a stroke.' (GB, p. 170).

The principle of simplicity is presented by Frege much more briefly than the principle of completeness; it is, however, less easy to understand, and it is formulated in two different ways which are not easy to reconcile.

In one formulation the principle is simply a provision that any symbol to be introduced by definition must be a simple symbol, in the sense of not having any parts which are themselves symbols. Of course any symbol or word will have physical parts, but this does not count against simplicity unless these parts have a role in the symbol system as independent signs with a meaning of their own. Thus, though the sign 'Socrates' contains the syllable 'rat' this does not count against its being a simple symbol, because that syllable is not playing the symbolic role of the word 'rat'. Frege gives a convincing reason for the principle, so understood: if the principle is violated, then it might happen that the parts were also defined separately and that these definitions contradicted the definition of the whole.

However, Frege also states his principle in a different way, which is more puzzling: 'we may not define a symbol or word by defining an expression in which it occurs, whose remaining parts are known' (GB, p. 170). It seems that what is prohibited here is a procedure which might well be applied to symbols which had no parts that were symbols, a procedure which therefore need not violate the principle of simplicity in its obvious form.

Frege gives two considerations in support of the principle, so stated. The first is that giving the reference of an expression and the reference of a part of it is insufficient to determine the reference of the remaining part. This is obviously true: I do not learn what the cube-function is by being told only that the value of the function is 27 for the argument 3; nor do I learn the meaning of the predicate '. . . is wise' by being told only that it expresses a concept which takes the value *True* for the argument Socrates. But this truth does not seem sufficient to establish the principle of simplicity, since it is concerned only with the reference of expressions, and not with their sense. What definition primarily establishes is a link between the sense, not the reference, of expressions; and we have been given no reason for ruling out the possibility of establishing the sense of part of an expression by explaining the sense of the whole and the sense of the remaining parts.

Frege's second consideration draws upon a metaphor. If we were to define a symbol in violation of this principle, he says,

it would first be necessary to investigate whether – to use a readily understandable metaphor from algebra – the equation can be solved for the unknown, and whether the unknown is unambiguously determined. But as I have already said above, it is not feasible to make the correctness of a definition depend on the outcome of such an investigation. (GB, p. 170.)

This seems to add little to what has gone before. In terms of the previous example, working out the equation corresponds to establishing that there *is* a function which takes the value 27 for the argument 3 (as there is) and that there is *only one* function which takes the value 27 for the argument 3 (as there is not). But once again we seem to be talking about reference when we should be talking about sense.

The algebraic metaphor is more compelling when it is used to caution against trying to define two things in a single definition, for instance to define the *equals* sign along with what stands to the right and left of it. 'One equation alone cannot be used to determine two unknowns.' (GB, p. 171).

We may wonder how the principle of simplicity, in its second form, squares with the principle of *The Foundations of Arithmetic* 'never to ask for the meaning of a word in isolation, but only in the context of a proposition'. Would Frege's own definition of number fall foul of his new principle?

There is, indeed, a general problem about applying Frege's principle of simplicity to the definition of functions.

Of course names of functions, because of their characteristic unsaturatedness, cannot stand alone on one side of a defining equation; their argument-places must always be filled up somehow or other. In my concept script, as we have seen, this is done by means of italic letters, which must then occur on the other side as well. In language, instead of these, there occur pronouns and particles ('something', 'what', 'it') which indicate indefinitely. This is no violation of our principle; for these letters, pronouns, particles do not stand for anything, but only indicate. (GB, p. 171.)

So in place of definitions of functions, Frege, in *Grundgesetze*, will offer equivalences between value-ranges. Indeed, the very first function which is defined by Frege, in the first volume, is one whose importance is derived from its role in his project of reducing statements about higher-level functions to statements about their value-ranges. The sign to be defined is '$\cap$': the expression '$x \cap z$' is intended to be a regimentation of the informal 'x is a member of z'. The definition reads as follows:

$$\vdash\!\!\!-/\grave{\alpha}(\neg\,(g)\,(u = \grave{\varepsilon}g(\varepsilon)) \to \neg(g(\alpha) = a) = \grave{\alpha} \cap u.$$

According to this definition, if we are given any object A and any function $\Phi(\xi)$, the expression '$A \cap \grave{\varepsilon}\Phi(\varepsilon)$' shall have the same reference as '$\Phi(A)$'; and secondly (to take care of waste cases) for any object D and any object G which is not a range the expression '$D \cap G$' shall be a name for the null class.[1]

Another function which might be substituted for $\Phi(\xi)$ is $\grave{\varepsilon}(\xi + \varepsilon)$. The values of this function are always value-ranges. The value-range of this function will then be a double value-range, say $\grave{\alpha}\grave{\varepsilon}(\alpha \geq \varepsilon)$. A double value-range of a two-place function which is a relation will count as the extension of that relation. Hence Frege can make use of his new notation when he comes to use properties of relations to construct numbers.

Frege now proceeds to define, with the help of his $\cap$ notation, a number of the functions which he used in *The Foundations of Arithmetic* in order to define number and individual numbers. First, in section 37 he introduces a sign for a relation's being a many–one relation, and in section 38 he recalls the definition in

---

1. W. and M. Kneale, *The Development of Logic*, Oxford University Press, 1962, p. 506.

Foundations of equivalence between concepts. He introduces the word 'map' to correspond with what a relation does when it correlates many–one the objects falling under the concept F with the objects falling under the concept G. If we call a concept whose extension is Γ, a Γ-concept, and a relation whose concept is Δ, a Δ-concept, and a relation whose extension is T, a T-relation, then we can say that the T-relation *maps* the Γ-concept into the Δ-concept. If two concepts are to be equivalent the mapping must be two-way; that is, not only must the T-relation map the first concept into the second, but the relation which is the converse of T must map the second concept into the first.

As in *Foundations*, Frege uses the concept of equivalence to define the number of the Γ-concept as the extension of the concept *equivalent to the* Γ-concept. He then goes on to define the number 0 as the number belonging to the concept whose extension is $\acute{\varepsilon}(\neg\varepsilon = \varepsilon)$, and the number 1 as the number belonging to the concept whose extension is $\acute{\varepsilon}(\varepsilon = 0)$. The successor relation and the ancestral relation are also defined, with minor alterations, in the same way as in *Foundations*.

Having set out the functions, inference rules and definitions of his system, Frege is now in a position to derive its theorem from its axioms. This he does in the third chapter.

The axioms, or basic laws, which give *Grundgesetze* its name, are given below in a modern symbolism, in which there is generally no need for Frege's judgement-strokes and horizontal strokes. The verbal equivalences given for each axiom are not exact, but are simply meant as hints to help the reader grasp Frege's intention.

I. $a \rightarrow b \rightarrow a$ (if a, then if b then a).

IIa. $(x)\, f(x) \rightarrow f(a)$ (what holds for every object holds for any particular object).

IIb. $(f)\, M_{\beta}(f(\beta)) \rightarrow M_{\beta}(f\beta)$ (what holds of every first-level one-argument function holds for any such function).

III. $g(a = b) \rightarrow (g[(f)fb \rightarrow fa])$. (There is a principle, sometimes called the indiscernibility of identicals, which says: if (i) a is identical with b, then (ii) whatever holds of b holds of a. This axiom says that if a function holds of (i) then it holds of (ii). Negation is a function, hence if (i) is false, then (ii) is false; this also gives us the identity of indiscernibles.)

IV. $\neg(-a = \neg b) \to (-a = -b)$ (if it is not the case that the truth-value of a is the same as the truth-value of not b, then a and b have the same truth-value; or, more approximately, if not p then p).

V. $(\grave{\varepsilon}f(\varepsilon) = \grave{\alpha}g(\alpha)) = ((x)\, f(x) = g(x))$ (if the value-ranges of two functions are identical, then the value of one function for a given argument is always the same as the value of the other function, and vice versa).

VI. $a = /\grave{\varepsilon}(a = \varepsilon)$ (an object A is the one and only thing which is identical with A).

These axioms are designed to introduce, in turn, the primitive signs: first the conditional, then the quantifiers for objects and functions, then the sign for identity, then that for negation, then that for value-ranges, and finally the description operator. From these axioms, by a limited and specified number of inference patterns, Frege undertakes to derive the whole of logic and arithmetic. The definitions which he has given, he maintains, supply no further basic material, but simply proofs to be abbreviated.

We noticed earlier that the apparatus of *Grundgesetze* does not really permit the definition of functions. In place of definitions of functions Frege offered equivalences between value-ranges. The use of this procedure is made possible by his axiom V, which allows the transformation of an equality holding generally between two functions into an identity between their value-ranges. So it must be asked how Frege's introduction of value-ranges stands up to his own rigorous canons of definition, as set out in the second volume of the work and as summarized above.

Frege constantly denied that objects could be created by definition. No mathematician should enumerate a list of properties and then say: I construct a thing that is to have these properties. But Frege denies that this is what his procedure amounts to: he is merely drawing attention to something which is in common between two functions which always have the same value for the same argument, and is giving the name 'value-range' to that common element. The transformation permitted by axiom V must not be regarded as a definition.

[N]either the word 'same', nor the word 'value-range': or a complex symbol like $\dot{\epsilon}\Phi(\epsilon)$, nor both together, are defined by means of it. For the sentence

the value-range of the first function is the same as the value-range of the second function

is complex, and contains as a part the word 'same', which must be regarded as completely known. Similarly, the symbol $\dot{\epsilon}\Phi(\epsilon) = \dot{\epsilon}\Psi(\epsilon)$ which is already known. (GB, p. 180.)

Frege immediately admits that if his introduction of the notion of value-range was intended as a definition, then it would violate his principle of simplicity. But it is wrong, he says, to regard the introduction of his primitive signs as definitions; for 'only what is logically complex can be defined; what is simple can only be pointed to'. He goes on to say that in introducing value-ranges he is not really doing anything different from what other mathematicians have done when they have spoken of two functions coinciding, or have spoken of the extensions of sets.

Frege is surely right to say that the explanation of value-ranges violates his canons of definition; but it is hard to see what right he has to deny that what he is offering is a definition. The notion of value-range is not a simple but a complex one, and the symbolism for it depends, in a way that the other basic symbols do not, on features of symbols already introduced.[2]

2. Though it must be said that, in the light of the interdefinability of the truth-functions, the notion of logical simplicity with which Frege is here operating is in any case a dubious one.

Frege, in denouncing other mathematicians' violations of his canons – their smuggling in two signs in a single definition, for instance – has this to say:

This twilight is needed by many mathematicians for the performance of their logical conjuring tricks. The ends that are meant to be achieved in this way are unexceptionably attained through our transformation of an equality that holds generally into an equality between ranges of values, by axiom 5. (GB, p. 172.)

But Frege's use of axiom 5, so far from turning twilight into daylight, was to cast his own whole system into darkness.

Towards the end of the first volume of *Grundgesetze*, Frege sets out in great detail his rules for inference: they make up a system which is much more complicated than that of *Concept Script*, but which permits swifter movement from axioms to theorems. There is no purpose to be served by listing them in detail, since they are formulated with an eye to the particular peculiarities of Frege's system. In so far as Frege's *Grundgesetze* is a systematization of formal logic, there are many more elegant ways of achieving his goal. Frege's own aim, of course, was not so much the formalization of logic, as the proof that arithmetic is derivable from these axioms, none of which appears to involve any element which is not purely logical. Again, it would serve no purpose to follow the course of the proofs he offered. For shortly before the publication of the second volume of the *Grundgesetze* it was discovered that there was a fatal flaw in the system.

In June 1902 Bertrand Russell, who was writing a book on the principles of mathematics in which he made considerable use of Frege's ideas, wrote to Frege pointing out an apparent contradiction in his system. He asked: suppose that w is the predicate '. . . is a predicate which cannot be predicated of itself?' Can w be predicated of itself? Whichever answer we give, we seem to reach an impasse. He went on to formulate a corresponding paradox about classes. It was this which, when it reached him, cast Frege into consternation. This is how Frege himself set out Russell's paradox.

Nobody will wish to assert of the class of men that it is a man. We have here a class that does not belong to itself. I say that something belongs to a class when it falls under the concept whose extension the class is. Let us now fix our eye on the concept: *class that does not belong to itself*. The extension of this concept (if we may speak of its extension) is thus the class of classes that do not belong to themselves. For short we will call it the class C. Let us now ask whether this class C belongs to itself. First, let us suppose that it does. If anything belongs to a class, it falls under the concept whose extension the class is. Thus if our class belongs to itself, it is a class that does not belong to itself. Our first supposition thus leads to self-contradiction. Secondly, let us suppose that our class C does not belong to itself; then it falls under the concept whose extension it itself is, and thus does belong to itself. Here once more we likewise get a contradiction. (GB, p. 235.)

Frege was justifiably downcast on receiving Russell's letter. His correspondence with Russell during the summer and autumn of 1902 shows the two philosophers casting around for a solution to the problem. Frege strove to maintain the fundamental lines of his system, and eventually thought he had found a way to repair it. In October he wrote a postscript to the second volume of *Grundgesetze*, then in press. The volume appeared in 1903 with the postscript, which began

Hardly anything more unfortunate can befall a scientific writer than to have one of the foundations of his edifice shaken after the work is finished.

This was the position I was placed in by a letter of Mr Bertrand Russell, just when the printing of this volume was nearing its completion. It is a matter of my Axiom (V). I have never disguised from myself its lack of the self-evidence that belongs to the other axioms and that must properly be demanded of a logical law. And so in fact I indicated this weak point in the Preface to Vol. I (p. vii). I should gladly have dispensed with this foundation if I had known of any substitute for it. And even now I do not see how arithmetic can be scientifically established; how numbers can be apprehended as logical objects and brought under review; unless we are permitted – at least conditionally – to pass from a concept to its extension.[3] May I always speak of the extension of a concept – speak of a class? And if not, how are the exceptional cases recognized? Can we always infer from one concept's coinciding in extension with another concept that any object that falls under the one falls under the other likewise? These are the questions raised by Mr Russell's communication. (BLA, p. 127).

Frege's axiom V, it will be recalled, was this:

$$(\grave{\varepsilon}f(\varepsilon) = \grave{\alpha}g(\alpha)) = ((x)f(x) = g(x)).$$

This tells us that if the value-ranges of two functions are identical, then the value of one function for a given argument is always the same as the value of the other function: we can make the passage from a class to the corresponding function. It also tells us, conversely, that if the value of one function for a given argument is always the same as the value of the other function for the same argument, then the value-ranges are identical: we can make the passage from a function to the corresponding class. Frege took Russell's paradox as showing that we cannot transform an identity of value-ranges into a general identity. It did not, however, he thought, undermine the possibility of transforming a general identity into an identity of value-ranges. Accordingly, he modified axiom V, so that it allowed the transition from a general identity at the level of function to an identity between classes, but it no longer allowed the corresponding transition between classes and functions. This weakening, he believed, would block the formulation of Russell's paradox, and yet allow arithmetic to be derived from logic as he proposed.

There is no need to set out Frege's modification to his system,

---

3. This was a point on which Frege had changed his mind. In *The Foundations of Arithmetic*, having defined the number which belongs to the concept *F* as the extension of the concept 'equivalent to the concept *F*', he adds, in a surprising footnote, 'I believe that for "extension of the concept" we could write simply "concept"' (FA, p. 80). He repeats this, without any recantation, in 'Concept and Object' (CP, p. 188). It is difficult to reconcile this insouciance with Frege's insistence that numbers are objects.

for it failed to achieve its purpose in two ways. In the first place, the weakening of the axiom invalidated the proofs of a number of important theorems, for instance the theorem that every natural number has a successor. In the second place, though Russell's paradox cannot be proved in the system, it is possible within the system (as the Polish logician Lesniewski showed in 1930) to prove that there are no two distinct objects, which is inconsistent with the thesis that the True and the False are two distinct objects.

Neither of these facts was known to Frege when the second volume of *Grundgesetze* was published, but it seems likely that he came to realize at least the first fact by 1906.[4] After that time he gave up writing on the foundations of mathematics until just before his death; he spoke in a letter about the complete failure which had attended his attempts to clarify the nature of number. He came even to abandon his fundamental idea that numbers were classes or sets. In an unpublished paper written in about 1924 he spoke of the temptation which language engenders in us to form proper names to which no objects correspond. He continued:

A particularly noteworthy example of this is the formation of a proper name after the pattern of 'the extension of the concept *a*', e.g. 'the extension of the concept *star*'. Because of the definite article, this expression appears to designate an object; but there is no object for which this phrase could be a linguistically appropriate designation. From this has arisen the paradoxes of set theory which have dealt the death blow to set theory itself. I myself was under this illusion when, in attempting to provide a logical foundation for numbers, I tried to construe numbers as sets. (PW, p. 269.)

In the last year of his life Frege returned to the Kantian position which he had set out to refute at the beginning of *The Foundations of Arithmetic*: since arithmetic was a priori, but had

4. I here follow the account given by Dummett in *Frege, Philosophy of Mathematics*, Duckworth, London, 1991, p. 6.

turned out not to be analytic, it must rest, like geometry, on intuition.

In his last paper, 'Numbers and Arithmetic', he talks with contempt of 'kindergarten-numbers' – the numbers that give the answer to the question 'How many', and to whose elucidation he had devoted the best years of his life. He once believed, he now tells us, that it was possible to conquer the entire number domain, continuing along a purely logical path from the kindergarten numbers; but he has now seen the mistake in this.

The more I have thought the matter over, the more convinced I have become that arithmetic and geometry have developed on the same basis – a geometrical one in fact – so that mathematics in its entirety is really geometry. Only on this view does mathematics present itself as completely homogeneous in nature. Counting, which arose psychologically out of the demands of business life, has led the learned astray. (PW, p. 277.)

CHAPTER 10

LOGICAL INVESTIGATIONS, I

Between 1918 and 1923 Frege published three articles in a German periodical, *Beiträge zur Philosophie des deutschen Idealismus*. Their titles can be translated as 'Thoughts', 'Negation' and 'Compound Thoughts'. They were intended as chapters of a book to be entitled *Logical Investigations* and in 1975 they were posthumously published together under this title.[1] They represent the most polished of several successive attempts which Frege made to present his mature philosophy of logic as a systematic whole. Several other drafts have survived and were also published posthumously. In what follows, I will follow the course of exposition of the published essays, but will supplement their argument from time to time with material from the uncompleted drafts.

These late essays are among the easiest to read of all Frege's writings. Symbolism rarely appears, and Frege's own concept script is totally absent. To anyone acquainted with twentieth-century analytical philosophy, the philosophical concerns appear more immediately familiar than those of the earlier and middle periods. Yet many of the main themes of the essays have formed part of Frege's teaching since the time of *Concept Script*.

This is true right from the beginning of the essay 'Thoughts', which is a renewed attack on psychologism in logic. The task of

---

1. *Logical Investigations*, edited with a preface by P. T. Geach; translated by P. T. Geach and R. H. Stoothoff, Oxford; Blackwell, 1977. The papers were republished as pp. 351–406 of CP, to which the references in this chapter and the next are given.

logic, Frege says, is to discern the laws of truth. But there are two kinds of laws: prescriptive and descriptive. Moral and civil laws prescribe what ought to be done; but people's actual behaviour often fails to accord with them. Laws of nature set out general features of natural events, and what happens cannot but be in accord with them. The laws of logic resemble laws of nature rather than civil laws, even though they lead to prescriptions about how one should think and infer.

Does logic deal with laws of thought? Here again we must distinguish. If we speak of logical laws as laws of thought, then we must mean the laws which, like the principles of morals or the laws of the state, prescribe how we are to act, and do not, like the laws of nature, define the actual course of events. Human beings' actual thinking does not always obey the laws of logic any more than their behaviour always obeys the moral law (PW, p. 145).

By 'laws of thought' we may, however, mean psychological laws describing mental processes and relating them to their causes. Any such law would not be a law of logic, because it would make no distinction between true thoughts and false thoughts: error and superstition have causes no less than sound belief.

The farmer whose fortunes are, for good or ill, bound up with the weather, seeks for means of determining what it will be like in advance. Little wonder that he attempts to link phases of the moon with variations in the weather and asks himself whether a full moon does not herald a change in the weather. If this appears to be confirmed . . . from that moment on he believes the weather is connected with the moon, and this belief takes root because the cases that speak in its favour make a greater impression than those that do not and imprint themselves more firmly on his memory; and he thinks he now knows this from experience. (PW, pp. 2–3.)

The success of the theory of evolution may lead us to question whether the laws of human thinking have evolved. Will an inference that is valid now still be valid after thousands of years, and was it valid thousands of years ago? (PW, p. 4.)

Clearly, this question involves a confusion between the laws of how people in fact think and the laws of valid inference. The task of logic is to discover the laws of truth, not the laws of thinking. Of course, once these have been discovered, they will provide both the basis for prescriptive laws of thought, and also perhaps an element in the causal explanation of actual mental processes (CP, p. 352).

Logic, then, deals with the laws of truth. So what is truth? Is it a property? Or is it a relation? Some thinkers have proposed that truth is a correspondence between a representation (a physical or mental picture, for example) and what it represents. But what a physical picture represents depends on the intention of its creator, which is something mental. Complete correspondence between a mental representation and a physical reality is impossible; so nothing could ever be completely true if truth were correspondence.

Moreover, if we define truth as any kind of relation or characteristic, the question can always be raised whether it is *true* that the representation in question possesses the specified characteristic or stands in the appropriate relation. 'And so we should be in the position of a man on a treadmill who makes a step forwards and upwards, but the step he treads on keeps giving way and he falls back to where he was before.' (PW, p. 134.) We must conclude that the content of the word 'true' is *sui generis* and indefinable (CP, p. 353).

The indefinability of truth is a theme common to Frege's writing, early and late. But in Frege's middle theory, truth was not a property of anything; rather, the True was an object which all true sentences named. Now he is willing to entertain once more the idea that truth is a property, albeit an indefinable one.

If truth is an indefinable property, what is it a property *of*? The truth or falsity of pictures and images – if we set aside the sense of 'truth' in which it is equivalent to 'authenticity' – boils down to the truth or falsehood of propositions expressing their content. So shall we say that it is the proposition that is the real bearer of truth? Well, a proposition is a series of sounds with a *sense*; and when we call a proposition true we really mean that its sense is true. The truth of a sentence is preserved when it is translated into the different sounds of a foreign language, and it is conceivable that the same set of sounds should be true in one language and false in another (PW, p. 129). There are some sentences that cannot be classified as true or false – commands, for instance. These have sense, but Frege denies that they express thoughts (CP, p. 355). A thought is the sense of an assertoric sentence or proposition. So it is the *thought* which is the primary bearer of truth and falsity; indeed that is what we mean by a thought, 'something for which the question of truth can arise at all'.

What more can we say about a thought, other than that it is a bearer of truth or falsity? First, it is imperceptible by the senses. It gets clothed, Frege says, in the perceptible garb of a sentence, and so we can get hold of it: the sentence *expresses* the thought. A philosopher who wishes to talk about thoughts cannot present them to his audience to handle, as a mineralogist can exhibit a rock-crystal: he has to present them wrapped up in a linguistic form (CP, p. 360).

If truth is a property of thoughts, and thoughts are imperceptible, then truth cannot be a sensible property, like a smell or taste or colour. But do we not see, for instance, that the Sun has risen, and therefore see that it *is true* that the Sun has risen? No: we see the risen Sun; but *that the Sun has risen* is not something we see, even though we accept it as true on the basis of what we see. If we do want to say that I see that a flower has five petals, then we are not using 'see' to record a visual experience; what we mean by it is bound up with thinking and judging (PW, p. 138). And there are many truths which are accepted not on the basis of sense-impressions; for example, that I do not smell anything at present. But this imperceptible property of imperceptible thoughts seems to be a strange one!

[T]he proposition 'I smell violets' has just the same content as 'It is true that I smell violets'. So it seems that nothing is added to the thought when I ascribe to it the property of truth. And yet is it not a great triumph when, after long uncertainty and laborious research, a scientist can finally say 'My hypothesis is true'? (CP, p. 354.)

Truth is so *sui generis* that perhaps it cannot really be called a property at all.

From time to time, Frege compares the predicate 'true' with the predicate 'beautiful'. Beauty, unlike truth, admits of degrees: one thing can be more beautiful than another. What is true is true independently of our recognizing it as true; what is beautiful is beautiful for the person who experiences it as such. When we claim objectivity for judgements about beauty, we are claiming that something would be felt to be beautiful by any normal human being, 'and each one of us cannot help but think that he himself is so close to the normal human being that he believes he can speak in his name' (PW, p. 132). But normality itself, Frege maintains, is relative to times and places. It is not so with truth.

At this point Frege restates a distinction familiar to readers of his earlier work: the distinction between thought and assertion. The sentences 'The door is open' and 'Is the door open?', Frege would say, have the same content and express the same thought, the thought of the door's being open; but the first sentence, in addition, asserts its content to be true, while the second, in addition, asks whether its content is true.[2] It is possible, clearly, to express a thought without declaring it to be true. It is equally possible to have a thought in one's mind without accepting it as true. We must therefore distinguish between three different operations: (1) thinking, the grasping of a thought; (2) judging, the mental acceptance of a thought as true; and (3) asserting, the public declaration that a thought is true.

---

2. Frege might have gone on to say that the sentence 'Open the door' also had the same content, but, in addition, commanded the content to be made true. Instead, but for no good reason, he denied that imperative sentences expressed thoughts.

To express an assertion the word 'true' is neither necessary nor sufficient. In real life the assertion '*p*' will achieve anything that the assertion '*p* is true' will achieve; and in make-believe situations, as on the stage, '*p* is true' will not be a real assertion any more than '*p*' will. Hence, again, nothing seems to be added to a thought by attributing to it the property of truth.

As often before, Frege distinguishes between a thought and what he calls the colouring of its expression. Scientific language as it were presents thoughts in black and white; but in humane disciplines sentences may clothe thoughts in colourful garb, with expressions of feeling, interjecting words and phrases like 'Alas!' or 'Thank God!' and using charged words like 'cur' instead of plain words like 'dog'. Such features of sentences do not affect their truth: a statement containing the word 'cur' in place of 'dog' does not become false merely because the person uttering it does not feel the hostility that the word expresses (PW, p. 140).

The more colourlessly scientific a text is, the easier it will be to translate from one language to another; the more poetic colour it has, the more difficult it will be to render faithfully. The grammar of natural languages is a mixture of the logical and the psychological; if this were not so, all languages would have the same grammar. This is what makes translation difficult, but it also means that the learning of different languages helps us to isolate the black-and-white logical sense from the different kinds of colouring with which it may be tinted. Colouring may be of extreme importance to the beauty of a sentence; but beauty is not truth, nor is truth beauty (CP, p. 356; PW, p. 142).

Some features of a sentence (for example, the use of a passive rather than an active verb) may serve for emphasis without affecting truth-value. Other features may relate the thought expressed by the sentence to other thoughts not expressed by it.

Someone using the sentence 'Alfred has not yet come' actually says 'Alfred has not come' and hints that his coming is expected. But this is only a hint; no one can say the sense of the sentence is false because Alfred's coming is not expected. (CP, p. 357.)

The point made by these illustrations is a familiar one: the content of a sentence often goes beyond the thought expressed by it.[3] But Frege now goes on to a point which has hitherto not been developed at any great length:

The mere wording, which can be made permanent by writing or the gramophone, does not suffice for the expression of the thought. (CP, p. 358.)

He has in mind the complications introduced by the tenses of verbs and by expressions such as 'today', 'here' and 'I'.

If a sentence contains a present tense used to indicate time (as in 'It is snowing') then you need to know when the sentence was uttered in order to grasp the thought expressed. 'Therefore', Frege says, not very happily, 'the time of utterance is part of the expression of the thought.' He goes on to say that something similar happens with the use of the first person pronoun. 'I am hungry' said by Peter expresses a different thought than is expressed by 'I am hungry' said by Paul. One may be true and the other false. It seems very odd to say, as Frege later does, that the person uttering a thought is a circumstance which forms part of the expression of the thought. However that may be, we have in both these sentences a case where one and the same sentence may, in different contexts, express a different thought.

The opposite can also happen, according to Frege. If on 9 December I say 'It was snowing yesterday' I express the same thought as if on 8 December I say 'It is snowing today'. He would presumably say the same about 'You are hungry' uttered by me, and 'I am hungry' uttered by you. Here we have the case where two different sentences may, at different times or in different mouths, express the same thought.

To illustrate the problem with the first-person pronoun, Frege

3. In the earlier terminology of *Concept Script* one might say that the content of a sentence includes more than its judgeable content.

presents a particularly complicated example, which we may present in a slightly simpler form. Let us suppose that a certain Dr Brian Smith says to one of his patients, Matthew, 'I have been wounded'. Three days later, Matthew says to his friends Mark, Luke and John, 'Brian Smith has been wounded.' Does this express the same thought as was expressed by Brian Smith himself three days earlier?

Frege does not give an immediate answer: instead he invites us to consider the thoughts in the minds of the hearers of the statement. What Matthew's friends understand by the sentence may depend on what each of them already knows. Mark, another patient of Dr Smith's, will understand the sentence in the same way as Matthew. But Luke, who knows nothing at all about Brian Smith, will not do so. Nor will John, who knows about Brian Smith only that he was the one person born in Balmoral Castle on 25 December 1898 – a fact which, as it happens, is unknown to Matthew. So, while Mark has the same thought about Brian Smith as Matthew has, John has a different thought, and Luke has no thought about him at all.

Frege says that two people situated as are Matthew and John do not speak the same language with respect to a proper name such as 'Brian Smith'. Although they do in fact refer to the same man by that name, they do not know they are doing so. Hence they both associate different senses with the sentence 'Brian Smith was wounded'. John might accept as true Matthew's statement 'Brian Smith was wounded' while not believing that *his* Brian Smith was wounded at all.

The conclusion which Frege draws from his complicated example is this:

Accordingly, with regard to proper names, it is a matter of importance how the object named is presented. This can happen in more than one way, and to each such way there corresponds a particular sense of a sentence containing the proper name. The different thoughts yielded by the same sentence must of course agree in truth-value: if one of them is true they are all true, and if one of them is false they all are. But the difference between them must be recognized. (CP, p. 359.)

If we want to avoid difficulties of this kind we will have to stipulate that for every proper name there should be just one associated mode of presentation of the named object.

Frege's conclusion may be regarded as a partial restatement of the distinction between sense and reference with which we have been familiar since 'Function and Concept'. But Frege now goes on to make a particular application of that distinction which takes him on to new, and dangerous, ground. He treats the first-person pronoun 'I' as a proper name, and inquires about the mode of presentation associated with it.

Everyone, Frege says, 'is presented to himself in a special and primary way, in which he is presented to no one else'. Consequently, when Dr Smith has the thought that he has been wounded, that thought will rest on this primary mode of self-presentation. Only he can grasp the sense of that thought, since it is only to himself that he can be presented in this special manner.

He cannot communicate a thought he alone can grasp. Therefore, if he now says 'I have been wounded' he must use 'I' in a sense which can be grasped by others, perhaps in the sense of 'the person who is now speaking to you'. In doing so he makes the circumstances of his utterance serve the expression of the thought. (CP, p. 360.)

The thought, therefore, which Dr Smith communicates to others is quite different from the one which he himself has.

Frege here reaches a conclusion which contradicts one of his own central theses. Throughout his life, when fighting for the distinction between psychology and logic, he had insisted that whereas mental images might be private, thoughts were the common property of us all. On his own principles, an incommunicable thought about a private ego would not be a thought at all. But instead of rejecting the whole notion of the Cartesian ego, he goes on to present in highly Cartesian terms a full-blown doctrine of two worlds, one exterior and public, and one interior and private.

Perceptible things of the physical world are accessible to us all: each of us can see the same houses and touch the same trees. But besides the outer world, Frege says, there is an inner world of sense-impressions, images and feelings, of desires and wishes. Let us, for present purposes, call all these items 'ideas'. Frege states four theses about ideas.

(1) Ideas are imperceptible. You cannot see my visual impressions: nor can I, they are not things I see, but things I have.

(2) Ideas belong to somebody. The frogs in the field exist whether I look at them or not; but there could not be a pain or a mood or a wish going round the world which was nobody's pain or mood or wish.

(3) Ideas need an owner. Much of what Frege says under this head seems simply to be a reinforcement of the point already made under the second head. If there is a new point to be made, it seems to be this: that belonging to a particular consciousness is not just a property which attaches to an independently identifiable idea, but is something which is essential to the identity of the idea itself. An idea is not simply like an atom which could not exist isolated and had to occur within some molecule, but yet could be identified as reappearing in several different molecules. (This possibility, perhaps, is left open by the second thesis.)

It is impossible to compare my sense-impression with someone else's. For that, it would be necessary to bring together in one consciousness a sense-impression belonging to one consciousness and a sense-impression belonging to another consciousness. Now even if it were possible to make an idea disappear from one consciousness and at the same time make an idea appear in another consciousness, the question whether it is the same idea would still remain unanswerable. It is so much of the essence of any one of my ideas to be a content of my consciousness, that any idea someone else has is, just as such, different from mine. (CP, p. 361.)

It is impossible for human beings to compare each other's ideas. I go into a strawberry patch. I pick a strawberry and hold it between my fingers. My companion and I see the same straw-berry; but, according to Frege, each of us has a different idea. This leads to his fourth thesis.

(4) Every idea has only one owner; no two human beings have the same idea.

Having delineated, by these theses, the characteristics of the world of ideas, Frege reaffirms his constantly asserted conviction that thoughts are not ideas. Other people, no less than I, can assent to Pythagoras' theorem. One cannot say of thoughts, as one can of ideas, that each thought requires an owner, and belongs to that owner's consciousness and to no other. If that were so there would be no such thing as science; only my science, and your science, and the separate science of Tom, Dick and Harry. So we must conclude that thoughts belong neither to the inner nor to the outer realm.

'A third realm', Frege concludes, 'must be recognized.' The denizens of this realm share with ideas the property of being imperceptible by the senses, and share with physical objects the property of being independent of an owner. Pythagoras' theorem is timelessly true and needs no owner; it does not begin to be true when it is first thought of or proved (CP, p. 362). As I do not create a tree by looking at it, I do not generate a thought by thinking; still less does the brain secrete thoughts, as the liver does gall (PW, p. 137).

Other people can grasp thoughts no less than I: we are not owners of our thoughts as we are owners of our ideas. We do not *have* thoughts as we have ideas; nor do we *perceive* thoughts as we see stars. Thoughts are what we *grasp*. What is grasped is already there and all we do is take possession of it. Of course, if a thought is grasped, there must be someone who is grasping it; but the person who does the grasping is the owner only of the thinking, not of the thought. No doubt, when a thinker grasps a thought, there is something in the thinker's consciousness which is aimed at the thought – perhaps, a mental image of a sentence expressing the thought. But this must not be confused with the thought itself.

Grasping a thought is quite different from creating a thought. Again, a thought's being true is quite different from my accepting it as true.

The work of science does not consist in creation, but in the discovery of true thoughts. The astronomer can apply a mathematical truth in the investigation of a long past event which took place when – on Earth at least – no one had yet recognized that truth. He can do this because the truth of a thought is timeless. Therefore that truth cannot have come to be only upon its discovery. (CP, p. 368.)

We can take possession of thoughts, and that might seem to count against their being timeless, but the thought is not changed in itself by being thus acted on, just as the Moon is unaffected whether we take any notice of it or not (PW, p. 138).

Thoughts, though objective and not subjective like ideas, are not causally active in the way in which objects are in the physical world. In that world, one things acts on another and changes it, is itself acted upon and itself changes. This is not so in the timeless world which Pythagoras' theorem inhabits.

But is not the thought that the tree is covered with green leaves a thought that will be false in six months' time – and does that not prove that there is change in the world of thoughts? Not so, says Frege. The sentence 'This tree is covered with green leaves' may become a false sentence; but this shows, at most, that the thought which it expresses may change. In reality the sentence lacks a time-specification, and therefore fails to specify a thought.

Only a sentence with the time-specification filled out, a sentence complete in every respect, expresses a thought. But this thought, if it is true, is true not only today or tomorrow, but timelessly. (CP, p. 370.)

What is eternal and unchangeable can neither act upon us nor be acted upon by us. But of course our grasp of a thought is something within time. This grasping is something inessential to the thought itself, but it has importance for us and for the world we live in. My grasping of Pythagoras' theorem and judging that it is true may lead me to make a decision which will bring about the acceleration of certain masses. Frege ends his essay on thoughts with one of his purple passages:

Could the great events of world history have come about without the communication of thoughts? And yet we are inclined to regard thoughts as inoperative, because they appear to be without influence on events, whereas thinking, judging, stating, understanding and the like are facts of human life. How much more effective a hammer appears compared with a thought! A hammer passes from one man's power to another, it is gripped, it undergoes pressure, and thus its density, the disposition of its parts, is locally changed. Nothing like this happens with a thought. When one person communicates it to another, it does not leave the control of the communicator; because in the last analysis human beings have no power over it. When a thought is grasped, at first it changes only the inner world of the person grasping it; it remains untouched in its essence, since the changes it undergoes involve only inessential properties. There is lacking here something we observe everywhere in physical processes: reciprocal action. Thoughts are not altogether inoperative, but their operation is quite different from that of things. Their effect is brought about by an activity of the thinkers; without this they would be inoperative, at least as far as we can see. And yet the thinker does not create them, but must take them as they are. They can be true without being grasped by a thinker; and they are not wholly inoperative even then, at least if they *could* be grasped and brought into operation. (CP, p. 371.)

'Thoughts' contains one of Frege's few sustained ventures into epistemology or theory of knowledge. Anyone who maintains, as Frege did in this essay, that our mental life takes place within an inner private world must at some time face the question: What reason is there for believing that there is any such thing as an outer world? Descartes, in his *Meditations*, uses sceptical arguments to purify the reader, temporarily, from belief in anything beyond the world of ideas; he then endeavours to restore the reader's faith in the external world by appeal to the truthfulness of God. Frege, in this essay, accepts the Cartesian distinction between matter (the world of things) and mind (the world of ideas). Like Descartes, he accepts the need to provide an answer to sceptical idealism, the thesis that nothing exists except ideas.

What if everything were only a dream, only a play performed on the stage of my consciousness? (CP, p. 363). I seem to be walking in a green field with a companion; but perhaps the realm of things is empty, and I only have ideas of which I myself am the owner. If only what is my idea can be the object of my awareness, then for all I know there is no green field (for a field is not an idea, and there are no green ideas) and no companion (for human beings are not ideas). For all I know there are not even any ideas other than my own (for I can know of no one else to own them). Can I even entertain the hypothesis that there are ideas other than my own? Even in judging there to be an idea not my own do I not make it into the object of my thinking, and therefore, into my idea?

Frege concludes:

Either the thesis that only what is my idea can be the object of my awareness is false, or all my knowledge and perception is restricted to the range of my ideas, to the stage of my consciousness. In this case I should have only an inner world and I should know nothing of other people. (CP, p. 364.)

Science offers no way out of this dilemma; on the contrary, it may lead to reinforced scepticism. A physiologist will explain how consciousness depends on nerve-fibres and ganglion-cells, how the visual impression of a tree is produced by light-rays refracted in the eye striking the visual nerve-endings and bringing about processes in the nervous system. Now provided the visual nerves are appropriately stimulated – whether by refracted light, or by electrical means – the idea of the tree will be produced whether or not the tree itself exists. Moreover, the stimulation of the visual nerve is not something given; it is an hypothesis. The visual impression may, for all we know, be capable of being caused by other means.

If we call what happens in our consciousness an idea, then we really experience only ideas, not their causes. And if the scientist wants to avoid all mere hypothesis, then he is left just with ideas; everything dissolves into ideas, even the light-rays, nerve-fibres and ganglion-cells from which he started. (CP, p. 365.)

If I follow this train of sceptical reasoning, I seem to be left with nothing but myself and my consciousness. But do I really encounter myself as something distinct from my ideas? Am I not myself an idea?

It seems to me as if I were lying in a deck-chair, as if I could see the toes of a pair of waxed boots, the front part of a pair of trousers, a waistcoat, buttons, parts of a jacket, in particular the sleeves, two hands, some hairs of a beard, the blurred outline of a nose. Am I myself this entire complex of visual impressions, this aggregate idea? (CP, p. 365.)

If so, if what I call 'I' is an idea, how is it different from other ideas, such as my idea of the chair over there? By what right do I pick out one of my ideas and set it up as owner of the others? Why have an owner for ideas at all? An owner would be something essentially different from ideas that are owned; but if everything is an idea, then there is no owner of ideas.

But here we come to a full stop. If there is no owner of ideas, there are no ideas either; dependence on an owner was one of the features by which the notion of 'idea' was introduced. There cannot be an experience without someone to experience, or a pain without someone who has it. Pain is necessarily *felt*, and what is felt must have someone feeling it. If so, there *is* something which is not my idea, and yet can be an object of my thought, namely, myself.

Frege, like Descartes, brings his sceptical train of thought to a halt with a *cogito, ergo sum*: I have ideas, therefore I am. In each case, the first non-ideal object whose existence is established is the self, the owner of the ideas, the substance in whom the *cogitationes* inhere. But there is a difference as well as a similarity. Frege distinguishes between my having an idea and my grasping a thought, whereas in Descartes' terminology I could register either of these activities with the verb '*cogito*'. For Frege the significance of the indubitability of the self is not so much that it provides a non-ideal subject to do my thinking, as that it provides a non-ideal object for me to think about. It refutes the thesis that only what belongs to the content of my consciousness can be the object of my thought.

When I state something about myself, my judgement concerns something which is not an idea. Moreover, my judgement need not be based upon an idea: when, for instance, I assert that I am not feeling pain at present. (Frege uses statements about the *absence* of pain to refute idealism about consciousness, just as he had used statements about the number zero to refute empiricism in mathematics.)

If I can think about myself, I can think about other people too. I can make statements about my brother which are not statements about my idea of my brother. If I can think about other people, I can think about other people's ideas. Two doctors may discuss the pain of one of their patients. Neither of them *has* the pain; only the patient has that. But for both of them the pain that they do not have is a common object of thought. They may, indeed, have an idea of the patient's pain, that is to say, some image they associate with the thought of the pain. Such an idea is indeed part of the doctors' consciousness; but it is not the object of their reflection or what they are trying to remove. The image, Frege says, is simply an aid to reflection, as a drawing may be (CP, p. 367).

Thought about things of which one is not the owner is essential if one is to have an environment. But, says the idealist sceptic, may not this be a mistake? May I not have gone wrong in thinking that my brother is an object of thought independent of my idea? Sure, says Frege, we do make mistakes. 'By the step with which I win an environment for myself I expose myself to the risk of error.' We can achieve certainty about the inner world, but only very great probability about the external world.

That the probability is indeed very high is shown by the existence of history, moral theory, religion and the sciences.

This final response to the idealist sceptic must strike any reader as extremely feeble. In agreeing that no statement about the external world is more than probable, Frege is conceding too much to the sceptic; in appealing to the validity of religion and science, Frege is asking the sceptic for concessions which he has no right to demand. Frege's response to Cartesian scepticism is no more convincing than Descartes' own response, which it resembles more than is immediately obvious. Both philosophers, having accepted a division between a public world of physical things and a private world of human consciousness, seek to join together what they have put asunder by making an appeal to a third world: the divine mind in the case of Descartes, and the world of objective thoughts in the case of Frege.

In each case the fatal mistake was the acceptance of the initial dichotomy. There are not two worlds, but a single one to which there belong not just inert physical objects, but also conscious, thinking, human beings. Frege was wrong, and sinned against his own cardinal principle of separating thoughts from ideas, in accepting that consciousness provides us with incommunicable contents and unshareable certainties. As Wittgenstein was later to demonstrate, the identification of even the most private elements of consciousness is essentially dependent on concepts which are developed for use in the one and only public world, in which we communicate by means of a shared language.

CHAPTER 11

LOGICAL INVESTIGATIONS, II

The essay 'Negation' of 1919 takes its start from the remark in 'Thoughts' that the very same thought occurs in a yes–no question as in an assertoric sentence which answers that question. Thus, for Frege, 'Did Caesar invade Britain?' has the same sense as 'Caesar invaded Britain' and contains the same thought.

In this example, the correct answer to the question is 'Yes'. But suppose we considered a question to which the correct answer was 'No', such as 'Did Caesar invade Ireland?' Then the thought which occurs in both sentences is a false one. But how can this be? If thoughts were subjective entities like ideas, there would be no problem about the existence of false thoughts. But, for Frege, a thought is something objective which individuals grasp but do not create. How then can there be false thoughts? If thoughts are objective, it is natural to think that a thought has being by being true. If so, then the expression 'false thought' is equivalent to 'non-existent thought'; and we could not say 'That three is greater than five is false', for the grammatical subject of this sentence would be empty. Similarly, 'Is three greater than five?' would have no sense.

In the case of the last question, we see immediately that the answer is no. But what of the question

$$\text{Is } (21/20)^{100} \text{ greater than } \sqrt[19]{(10^{21})}?$$

Here, whether the question has a sense or not seems to depend on its answer, which is yet to be worked out. But it must surely be possible to grasp the sense of a question before answering it;

otherwise no answer would be possible at all. Or, if we approach the matter from the other direction, if truth was part of the content of an interrogative sentence, then in grasping the sense of the sentence I would see that it was true. Asking a question would be answering it. So we must abandon the suggestion that the being of a thought consists in its being true. There are such things as false thoughts.

Thoughts that perhaps turn out later on to be false have a justifiable use in science, and must not be treated as having no being. Consider indirect proof; here knowledge of the truth is attained precisely through our grasping a false thought. The teacher says 'Suppose *a* were not equal to *b*'. A beginner at once thinks, 'What nonsense! I can see that *a* is equal to *b*'; he is confusing the senselessness of a sentence with the falsity of the thought expressed in it. (CP, p. 375.)

The teacher in Frege's example is likely to go on to draw out the consequences of the false supposition, and show that they lead to a contradiction. Then, by *reductio ad absurdum*, the teacher will conclude that the initial supposition is false, and that *a* is indeed equal to *b*.

   Throughout his life, for no obvious reason, Frege insisted that nothing could be inferred from a false thought. He repeats this doctrine at this point, but goes on to say that a false thought can be part of a true thought, from which inference is possible. He requires that false propositions should occur in proofs only as unasserted elements of asserted compound propositions. The teacher should therefore not say, 'Suppose *a* is not equal to *b*, then it follows that *p* and not *p*, therefore, *a* is equal to *b*,' but rather, 'If *a* is not equal to *b*, then *p* and not *p*, but not (*p* and not *p*), therefore, *a* is equal to *b*.' In fact, given an appropriate system of rules, indirect proof can be carried out in either way, with equal legitimacy. In complicated cases, Frege's method leads to proofs that are extremely cumbrous. He clearly regarded the matter not merely as a choice between different formalisms, but as a substantial issue in the philosophy of logic. In this he seems to have been mistaken. There is nothing wrong with saying that a thinker's inferences were impeccable, but his premisses were false.

The method preferred by Frege involves regular use of the procedure of contraposition, that is to say, of inferring from a proposition of the form 'if p then q' to a proposition of the form 'if not q then not p'. This procedure has in any case been familiar to logicians for centuries. Frege observes that anyone who admits the legitimacy of this transition must accept that false thoughts have being. Otherwise, if p and q are both true, then the conclusion of the inference is entirely void; and if only one of p and q is true, then each of the propositions involved in the inference will lack either an antecedent or a consequent.[1]

Rather than saying that the being of a thought consists in the thought's being true, we should say that it lies in the possibility of different thinkers grasping the thought as one and the same thought. In this sense, too, we must admit that false thoughts do have being. Otherwise, it would be impossible, among other things, for a team of researchers ever to establish a negative result. Once research had established, for instance, that bovine tuberculosis was not communicable to humans, the very hypothesis under investigation, 'Bovine tuberculosis is communicable to humans', would be shown to have lacked any meaning common to each of the researchers.

Trial by jury presupposes that each juror can understand the question at issue in the same sense. In the course of a trial, it may be that the jurors are told, truly, 'If the accused was in Rome at the material time, he did not commit the murder.' Suppose it is false that the accused was in Rome. Then, according to the thesis that false thoughts have no publicly graspable sense, we would have to say that each juror could grasp the same thought in the whole sentence, and yet associate with the *if*-clause a private sense of his own.

---

1. Frege's exposition of this simple point (CP, p. 377) appears confused and incomplete; it seems possible that something is missing from the printed text.

False thoughts, Frege concludes, are indispensable. They are indispensable above all in connection with negation.

It must be possible to negate a false thought, and for this I need the thought; I cannot negate what is not there. And by negation I cannot transform something that needs me as its owner into something of which I am not the owner, something which can be grasped by several people as one and the same thing. (CP, p. 377.)

According to a long-standing logical tradition, negation involves some form of division. In the terminology of the medieval schoolmen, for instance, 'composition' and 'division' were almost synonyms for 'affirmation' and 'negation'. Frege asks, 'Is the negation of a thought to be regarded as a dissolution of the thought into its component parts?'

This suggestion has only to be clearly contemplated in order to be rejected. Our act of judgement cannot alter the make-up of a thought. An act of judging does not make a thought or put its parts in order, nor can another act of judgement break up the interconnection of the parts (CP, p. 382). A jury's negative verdict does not dissolve the thought expressed by the charge into mere fragments of thought. Inserting a 'not' into a true sentence does not turn it into the expression of a non-thought. The resulting sentence can be quite justifiably used as the clause of a conditional. Likewise, inserting a 'not' into a false sentence does not have the effect of turning a non-thought into a thought.

When we negate a sentence, we insert a 'not' at some suitable point, or preface the sentence with 'It is not the case that ...'; we leave the sentence otherwise intact, with its original order unaltered. This is quite different from dismantling the sentence, say by cutting it into word-length scraps to be shuffled about or carried away by the wind. The negation of a thought, similarly, is something quite different from the separation or dissolution of its elements.

This comes out particularly clearly in the case of double negation. From the sentence

The Schneekoppe is higher than the Brocken.

I get by simple negation

The Schneekoppe is not higher than the Brocken.

A double negation gives

It is not the case that the Schneekoppe is not
higher than the Brocken.

If negation was dissolution, then after the first negation we should have only fragments of a thought.

We should then have to suppose that the second negation could put these fragments together again. Negation would thus be like a sword that could heal on again the limbs it had cut off. But here the greatest care would be wanted. The parts of the thought have lost all connexion and inter-relation on account of its being negated the first time. So by carelessly employing the healing power of negation, we might easily get the sentence 'The Brocken is higher than the Schneekoppe'. (CP, p. 379.)

What indeed are the objects which negation is supposed to separate? They are not parts of sentences, nor are they parts of thoughts. Are they things in the world? Things in the world do not bother about our negating. Are they, then, mental images? If so, negation would be a private act, different for each of us; there would be no possibility of common verdicts of not guilty. 'It thus appears impossible to state what really is dissolved, split up, or separated by the act of negation.'

Aquinas, who was well aware of Frege's point, but who also made use of the terminology of 'composition' and 'division', gave the following answer to the question: What gets divided in a negative judgement?

If we consider the state of affairs in the mind on its own, there is always putting together where there is truth and falsehood; these are never to be found in the mind unless the mind puts one non-complex thought next to another. But if thoughts are considered in their relation to reality, they are sometimes called *compositio* and sometimes *divisio*.

They are called *compositio* when the mind puts one idea next to another as a way of grasping the putting together or identity of the things they are ideas of; they are called *divisio* when the mind puts one idea next to another as a way of grasping that the things are diverse.[2]

Translated into the terms of Frege's system, this may be regarded as tantamount to saying that the things that are put together in an affirmative judgement, and set asunder in a negative judgement, are the thought and the True.

But in these late essays Frege does not introduce the objects the True and the False,[3] though he repeats, as often before, that the term 'true' is indefinable. Moreover, unlike Aquinas, he feels no need to make room for negative judgements or acts of negation. For Frege, there is no need to introduce denial as a polar opposite of assertion. Negations belong with the thought asserted, and to deny the proposition that *p* is simply to assert that not *p*. The idea of an act of negation as a polar opposite of judging is an attempt to fuse together the act of judging with the negation that is a component of a thought. It is the latter to which there corresponds, in ordinary language, the word 'not' as part of the predicate (CP, p. 382).

If we were to admit denial as a polar opposite of, or a special kind of, assertion we would get into difficulty in accounting for some quite simple forms of inference. To accommodate them we would have to complicate our rules of inference intolerably. Consider the argument:

> If the accused was not in Berlin at the time of the murder, he did not commit the murder.

2. *In Libros Peri Hermeneias* (ed. Spiazzi, Turin, 1955), 1, 3, 26.

3. Indeed, he seems in this essay to regard sentences not as names of truth-values, but as names of thoughts. He writes (CP, p. 387), 'The definite article "*the*" in the expression *the* negation of the thought that 3 is greater than 5 shows that this expression is meant to designate a definite single thing. This single thing is in our case a thought. The definite article makes the whole expression into a singular name, a proxy for a proper name.'

The accused was not in Berlin at the time of the murder.
So, the accused did not commit the murder.

If we treat the premises and the conclusion as each being assertions, then the inference is a case of the familiar *modus ponens*. But if we are to treat negation as belonging to the act of judgement rather than as a component of the content of a judgement, then we have to regard the argument as constructed in the following manner:

> Asserted: If not *p* then not *q*.
> Denied: *p*.
> So: Denied: *q*.

Now we do not have the assertion of a conditional conjoined with the assertion of its antecedent leading to the assertion of its consequent here; instead we have the assertion of a conditional followed by the denial of a proposition which differs from the antecedent of the conditional, and this assertion and denial lead to the denial of a proposition which differs from the consequent of the conditional. In order to provide for inferences of this and similar kinds, we would have to construct an intolerably complicated set of rules. It is far preferable to accept that negation belongs with the thought asserted, and to treat denial as simply the assertion of the negation of a thought. Every thought has a contradictory thought, and we accept the falsity of a thought by assenting to the truth of a contradictory.

But to say that negation belongs with the thought asserted is not to say that there are positive and negative thoughts.

Consider the sentences 'Christ is immortal', 'Christ lives for ever', 'Christ is not immortal', 'Christ is mortal', 'Christ does not live for ever'. Now which of the thoughts we have here is affirmative, which negative? (CP, p. 380.)

Because the sign of negation in ordinary language is closely united to the predicate, it may seem that what is negated is not an entire thought, but just part of the thought. This temptation is already there in a sentence like 'Socrates is not wise'; it is even stronger in the case of sentences like 'Socrates is unwise'. But Frege insists that in such cases by combining a negative symbol with part of a sentence we negate the content of the whole sentence.

For him what is negated must be something capable of being a whole sentence. But of course, when it is negated, it becomes part of a larger whole. 'It is not the case that *p*' is made up of '*p*' and the sign of negation.

The thought does not, by its make-up, stand in any need of completion; it is self-sufficient. Negation on the other hand needs to be completed by a thought. The two components, if we choose to employ this expression, are quite different in kind and contribute quite differently towards the formation of the whole. One completes, the other is completed. (CP, p. 386.)

Readers of Frege's earlier works quickly see that he is here stating, without his formal terminology, that negation is a function, and as such, unsaturated. (In a subsequent essay, 'Compound Thoughts', he does indeed call negation an unsaturated part of a thought.) Negation is, of course, a truth-function, the most elementary such function.

Frege says 'To bring out in language the need for completion, we may write "The negation of . . .", where the blank after "of" indicates where the completing expression is to be inserted. For the relation of completing, in the realm of thoughts and their parts, has something similar corresponding to it in the realm of sentences and their parts.' Here we recognize an echo of the theory of linguistic functions enunciated in the *Concept Script*.

Negation is unusual in being a function which can be applied to something that is a value of itself. Double negation (as in 'It is not the case that it is not the case that *p*') can be regarded either as the result of taking '*p*' as the argument of the function 'It is not the case that it is not the case that . . .', or as taking 'it is not the case that *p*' as the argument of the function 'It is not the case that . . .' Corresponding to these two different ways of structuring the sentence, there are two ways of regarding the structure of the thought expressed by it.

Frege offers a comparison between a function and a piece of clothing. A coat cannot stand up by itself; it can stand up only if worn by someone. A man wearing a coat may put a cloak on top. We can say either that a man wearing a coat is now wearing a second wrapping; or that a man is wearing a wrapping consisting of a coat plus a cloak. Either way of looking at the matter, Frege says, is equally justified. And he concludes with the observation that clothing a thought in double negation does not alter its truth-value.

In the last of these three essays, 'Compound Thoughts', Frege passes from negation to the other elementary truth-functions. In this essay he lists six different kinds of what he calls 'compound thoughts'.

Conjunction, like negation, is seen by Frege as something which is to operate upon unasserted sentences; if we assert '*p* and *q*' this is to be seen as a single assertion of a compound sentence, not a pair of assertions joined by 'and'.

In giving his truth-functional explanation of 'and' Frege has a passage which illuminates his view, in this final period of his life, of the relationship between linguistic functions (unsaturated signs) and what corresponds to these functions in the realm of sense.

The 'and' whose mode of employment is more precisely delimited in this way seems doubly unsaturated: to saturate it we require both a sentence preceding and another following. And what corresponds to 'and' in the realm of sense must also be doubly unsaturated: inasmuch as it is saturated by thoughts, it combines them together. As a mere thing, of course, the group of letters 'and' is no more unsaturated than any other thing. It may be called unsaturated in respect of its employment as a symbol meant to express a sense, for here it can have the intended sense only when situated between two sentences: its purpose as a symbol requires completion by a preceding and a succeeding sentence. It is really in the realm of sense that unsaturatedness is found, and it is transferred from there to the symbol. (CP, p. 393.)

This passage is important in relating the unsaturatedness of a symbol to the purpose or use of a symbol. The notion of unsaturatedness is lifted from the realm of metaphysics to the area of linguistic usage.

Frege says that 'B and A' has the same sense as 'A and B'. In ordinary language there may seem to be a big difference between

> He drove his car home and drank half a litre of vodka

and

> He drank half a litre of vodka and drove his car home,

but Frege is treating 'and' as a truth-functional connective, so that 'p and q' is true if and only if 'p' is true and 'q' is true. No doubt he would say that the indication of temporal sequence in the quoted sentences is a matter of something that is hinted, rather than stated, or perhaps something belonging to the 'colour' of thoughts, like the difference between 'and' and 'but'.

The five kinds of compound thought listed by Frege in addition to 'A and B' are as follows:

II. not (A and B); III. (not A) and (not B);
IV. not ((not A) and (not B)); V. (not A) and B;
VI. not ((not A) and B).

There is no need to follow in detail his exposition of each of these kinds of thought, with their obvious truth-conditions. The third is equivalent to 'Neither A nor B', and the fourth is equivalent to 'A or B', understood non-exclusively, that is, as not ruling out the possibility that both A and B are true. A compound of the sixth kind, which is false if and only if the first component is true and the second is false, is equivalent to 'if B then A', understood truth-functionally.

Frege repeats for other kinds of thought the remarks he made about the unsaturatedness of conjunction. In 'neither A nor B' the connective is the sense of everything in the expressions apart from the letters 'A and B'. The two gaps in 'neither . . . nor . . .'

indicate the twofold unsaturatedness of these expressions which corresponds to the twofold unsaturatedness of the connective.

He emphasizes that the truth-functional interpretation of the connectives, though essential for scientific purposes, leads to odd-sounding results in ordinary language. For instance, the following sentences come out true:

> Frederick the Great won the battle of Rossbach, or two is greater than three.
> If I own a cock which has laid eggs today, then Cologne Cathedral will collapse tomorrow morning.

In everyday conversation we expect the sense of two sentences conjoined by 'or' or 'if' to have a connection with each other; but on the account which Frege gives of the connectives no such connection is required. Frege says, about the second sentence,

Questions of all kinds arise at this point, e.g. the relation of cause and effect, the intention of a speaker who utters a sentence of the form 'If *B*, then *A*', the grounds on which he holds its content to be true. The speaker may perhaps give hints in regard to such questions arising among his hearers. These hints are among the adjuncts which surround the thought in ordinary language. My task here is to remove the adjuncts and thereby to pick out, as the logical kernel, a compound of two thoughts which I have called a hypothetical compound thought. (CP, p. 401.)

In 'Compound Thoughts' the various possible truth-functions of two arguments are built up from negation and conjunction as primitives. This differs from the system of *Concept Script*, where the truth-functional conditional rather than conjunction was taken as primitive. Frege alludes to this possibility at the end of the essay. Some of the compounds may seem psychologically more natural than the others, but logically they are all on a par with each other. Thus we could start with a sentence containing only 'if' and 'not', 'If *B* then not *A*'; and if we negate this we get 'Not (if *B* then not *A*)'. This is equivalent to '*A* and *B*'. All six compound thoughts could be derived in a similar way from hypothetical compounds and negation.

Frege leaves open the question whether there are compound thoughts formed in any other way than truth-functionally. Physics, chemistry and astronomy, he conjectures, will be likely to resemble mathematics; but 'in order that' clauses call for caution and seem to require more investigation.

Frege ends the essay with the assertion that the only kind of compound thoughts needed for mathematics will be thoughts compounded from conjunction and negation in the matter explained. All mathematical thoughts are therefore built up truth-functionally. If one component of a mathematical compound thought is replaced by another thought having the same truth-value, then the resultant compound thought has the same truth-value as the original.

This thesis would be entailed by Frege's earlier logicist thesis, but it can be true independently of it, since it leaves open the question whether the primitive propositions out of which mathematical propositions are compounded are known by special mathematical intuition, or are basic truths of logic.

'Compound Thoughts' was the last thing Frege published; he had only two years more to live. His project of presenting in an informal and philosophical manner the logical system which he had developed in *Concept Script* and its successors was never completed. Had he continued, the next chapter would no doubt have explained, for the non-mathematical public, the operation of the quantifiers and the scope of the predicate calculus. It is sad that he did not live to write it, and so we do not have his final thoughts abut the greatest of his contributions to logic.

CHAPTER 12

FREGE'S ACHIEVEMENT

Frege often compared the mathematician to a geographer who explores new continents. His own career as a thinker resembled the career of exploration of Christopher Columbus. Just as Columbus failed in his project of discovering a westward passage to India, but unknowingly made Europe acquainted with a whole new continent, so Frege failed in his task of deriving arithmetic from logic, but made discoveries in logic and advances in philosophy which permanently changed the whole map of both subjects. Like Columbus, Frege failed to appreciate the full value of his own genuine discoveries, and he suffered discouragement and depression in consequence.

Frege devoted the best years of his life to proving the continuity between arithmetic and logic. All the other innovations of his fertile mind were intended to serve that overarching purpose, and when the project aborted it was natural that he should be tempted to think that his life's work had been a failure.

We now know that the logicist programme cannot ever be successfully carried out. The path from the axioms of logic to the theorems of arithmetic is barred at two points. First, as Frege himself learnt from the failure of his attempts to cope with Russell's paradox, the naïve set theory which was part of the system's logical basis was irremediably inconsistent in itself. Thus, the axioms of arithmetic could not be derived from purely logical axioms in the way he hoped. Secondly, the notion of 'axioms of arithmetic' was itself called in question after Frege's death when the Austrian logician Kurt Gödel showed that it was impossible to give arithmetic a complete and consistent axiomatization.

None the less, the calculi, concepts and insights developed by Frege in the course of expounding his logicist thesis have a permanent interest which is unimpaired by the defeat of that programme. He showed a remarkable insight into the enduring elements of his logical work in a diary entry in August 1906 – at what must have been the height of his depression over the disaster which overtook the *Grundgesetze* – entitled 'What may I regard as the result of my work?' The note is worth reproducing in full.

It is almost all tied up with the concept-script, a concept construed as a function. [A] relation as a function of two arguments. [T]he extension of a concept or class is not the primary thing for me. [U]nsaturatedness both in the case of concepts and functions. [T]he true nature of concept and function recognized.

[S]trictly I should have begun by mentioning the judgement-stroke, the dissociation of assertoric force from the predicate . . .

Hypothetical mode of sentence composition . . .

Generality . . .

Sense and reference. (PW, p. 184.)

All the items mentioned here have either long passed into the common patrimony of logicians, or are topics of contemporary philosophical debate to which Frege's writings are still of the utmost relevance.

We may consider in turn Frege's contribution as a logician, as a philosopher of logic and as a philosopher of mathematics. Frege was right to list the concept script as the first of his unassailable achievements. His pamphlet of 1879 marked an epoch without parallel in the history of logic. Within some hundred pages it presented the first ever comprehensive system of the main areas of logic. The propositional calculus (which Frege is alluding to in his note by 'hypothetical mode of sentence composition') and the functional calculus (the treatment of 'generality') contained in the *Concept Script* have a permanent place at the heart of modern logic. As two distinguished historians of logic have put it, 'it is no exaggeration to say that the use of quantifiers to bind variables was one of the greatest intellectual inventions of the nineteenth century'.[1]

If Aristotle was the founder of logic, Frege refounded it, and logic has developed faster and further in the period between his time and the present day than it did in all the centuries which separated him from Aristotle. It is true that the philosophers, mathematicians and information scientists who share a common elementary logic course will, in their logical researches, have little more in common than a psychologist and a quantum physicist who have shared an elementary statistics course; but the primitive foundation on which all their work is built will be the calculi devised by Frege. The invention of mathematical logic was, of course, one of the major contributions to the developments in many disciplines which resulted in the invention of computers. Thus, Frege's work as a logician has an effect today on the lives of ordinary people throughout the world.

In the course of his work, as we have seen, in addition to propositional and functional calculus, Frege developed other branches of logic, including second-order predicate calculus and a version of naïve set theory. His influence in logic has reached far beyond the areas which he had himself developed systematically. In those areas his influence was transmitted principally by the volumes of Russell and Whitehead's massive *Principia Mathematica* (though this work in some ways falls short of the philosophical clarity of his own works). Since that time there has been enormous progress in the areas of logic which Frege had studied: among early and significant developments were the perfection of non-axiomatic methods of handling propositional and functional calculus, and the establishment of formal semantics to match the standards of rigour which Frege had introduced into formal syntax.

1. W. and M. Kneale, *The Development of Logic*, Oxford University Press, 1962, p. 511.

Frege did not explore the areas of logic known as modal logic (that part of logic that deals with necessity, possibility and kindred notions) or tense logic (the logic of temporal or significantly tensed statements). These branches of logic had been studied in the Middle Ages, and have been studied again in the present century in the light of his innovations. His own predominantly mathematical agenda made him comparatively uninterested in the branches of logic which concern inferences about the transient and the changing.

Frege's diary note quoted above lists four of his results in the philosophy of logic. Three of them – the dissociation of assertoric force from predication, the treatment of concepts as functions and of relations as functions of two arguments – are solid and enduring achievements; though contemporary philosophers are no more certain than Frege was himself how best to present in non-metaphorical terms the insight that lies behind calling a function 'unsaturated'. The fourth, the distinction between sense and reference, is the ancestor of currently popular theories of meaning according to which the sense of a word is the contribution it makes to determining the truth-value of sentences in which it occurs. All these items listed by Frege are, indeed, enduring advances in the philosophy of logic.

However, the most important of Frege's irreversible achievements does not figure in his list: this was his separation of logic from psychology and epistemology. The Cartesian tradition had placed epistemology in the forefront of philosophy; the empiricist tradition had confused the study of logic with an inquiry into human mental processes. Frege disentangled logic from psychology, and gave it the place in the forefront of philosophy which had hitherto been occupied by epistemology. It is this fact which, more than any other, allows Frege to be regarded as the founding father of modern analytic philosophy.

Michael Dummett has put the matter thus:

What distinguishes analytical philosophy, in its diverse manifestations, from other schools is the belief, first, that a philosophical account of thought can be attained through a philosophical account of language, and, secondly, that a comprehensive account can only be so attained.[2]

If, therefore, analytical philosophy was born when the 'linguistic turn' was taken, its birthday must be dated to the publication of *The Foundations of Arithmetic* in 1884 when Frege decided that the way to investigate the nature of number was to analyse sentences in which numerals occurred.

In listing his achievements, Frege does not mention his work as a philosopher of mathematics. This is unsurprising, since at the time when he was writing his diary it appeared to be in ruins. It is, indeed, true that Frege's philosophy of mathematics has dated in a way in which his philosophy of logic has not. And yet, historians of philosophy commonly regard him as the greatest philosopher of mathematics there has ever been.

This is not as paradoxical as it sounds. The measure of Frege's greatness as a philosopher of mathematics is that his work completely antiquated everything previously written. No one can now take seriously the work of even the greatest previous writers on the subject. Frege's own positive account of the nature of number was, as he was aware, tragically flawed; but no one henceforth could write on the topic without taking his work as a starting point.

Frege's work in philosophical logic was not completely without precedent in this way. Many of his insights – such as the distinction between assertion and predication – were well appreciated by scholastic philosophers, though they had been obscured in the intervening period. His theory that functions are the reference of predicates resembles in several ways Aquinas's explanation of predication in terms of individualized forms. In distinguishing logic from psychology he was in line with a tradition originating with Aristotle's *De Interpretatione*; and of course when he made logic, rather than epistemology, the

2. M. Dummett, *Origins of Analytical Philosophy*, p. 4.

foundational discipline of philosophy he was restoring it to the place which it had had in the Middle Ages.

For most of his life, Frege gave priority to logic simply by ignoring epistemology. It was only in his final period, after the diary entry which we have taken as our text, that he turned his attention directly to epistemological questions. As we have seen, his efforts here cannot be regarded as successful in dissolving the problems with which epistemologists had wrestled. His attempt to set up a triple world of experience, thought and physics was a blind alley. While rejecting the subjectivity of thought, he accepted uncritically the Cartesian view of the subjectivity of experience, regarding sensations and images as essentially private and incommunicable experiences.

In the decades after Frege's essay, 'Thoughts', Wittgenstein developed a series of arguments to show that the identification of even the most private elements of consciousness is essentially dependent on concepts which are developed for use in the public world in which we communicate by means of a shared language. His work can be thought of, in one way, as an extension of Frege's campaign against psychologism. Agreeing with Frege that thoughts are common property, Wittgenstein went on to show, against Frege, that not even ideas are private in the sense of being incommunicable.

Anyone who has come to appreciate the force of Wittgenstein's celebrated arguments against private languages will see Frege's epistemology as fundamentally flawed. Indeed, it seems probable that the theses of Frege's later work provided much of the target of Wittgenstein's attack. But Wittgenstein's achievement is in part due to the work of Frege. The Cartesianism which was widespread when Frege wrote involved an erroneous conception of both thought and ideas. Frege exposed Cartesian errors about thought, while retaining, and expressing in a particularly candid manner, Cartesian errors about ideas. It is as if the residual Cartesian poison running through the philosophical systems of the day was gathered by Frege in this essay into a single virulent boil ready to be lanced by Wittgenstein.

Wittgenstein, throughout his life, owned an enormous debt to Frege. In his early work, the *Tractatus Logico-Philosophicus*, he rightly acknowledges his indebtedness to 'the great works of Frege'. Even in his posthumously published later works, which undercut some of Frege's cherished doctrines, Wittgenstein remained much influenced by Frege's agenda and by Frege's structures of thought.

One debt which Wittgenstein explicitly acknowledged was a debt to Frege's style. 'The style of my sentences', he wrote, 'is extraordinarily strongly influenced by Frege. And if I wanted to, I could establish this influence where at first sight no one would see it.'[3] Frege's mastery of style was indeed not the least of his remarkable gifts as a philosopher. *The Foundations of Arithmetic*, in particular, is one of the great philosophical masterpieces of all time: original, lucid, vigorous, economical, witty, subtle and profound. These qualities are rarely combined in the works of even the greatest philosophers, and as a philosophical stylist Frege has been surpassed only by Plato and Descartes. Like them, and beyond all other philosophers, he possessed the gift of writing prose which is accessible and attractive on first acquaintance and yet which repays rereading over a lifetime.

3. L. Wittgenstein, *Zettel*, Oxford, Blackwell, 1967, 712.

FREGE'S SYMBOLIC NOTATION

Frege's symbolic notation, first set out in *Concept Script* and used, with minor modification, for *Grundgesetze der Arithmetik*, is now never used. Instead, most logicians use the system devised by Peano in 1894 and adopted by Russell and Whitehead in their *Principia Mathematica* of 1910. There are several variants of this system, one of which has been used in the present book.

Formulas of Frege's system are not written in the linear manner of Peano's system. Instead, they form a two-dimensional array. This is because the symbol for the truth-functional conditional, corresponding to '*p* → *q*', which is basic to the construction of his formulae has the following form:

$$\begin{array}{l} \underline{}\; q \\ \underline{}\; p \end{array}$$

Thus the first of Frege's axioms has the form:

This would now be read as 'if *p*, then if *q* then *p*'. Frege uses italic letters from the beginning of the alphabet both as dummy names and as propositional variables or, as he would say, to indefinitely indicate individuals and truth-values. (In his later work this is, of course, connected with his thesis that a sentence refers to a truth-value in just the same way as a proper name refers to an individual.) It is now customary to use letters from the beginning of the alphabet to take the place of names, and to use letters such as 'p', 'q' and 'r', as propositional variables.

To symbolize the universal quantifier Frege uses a Gothic letter over a concavity in the horizontal line which he uses as a content-stroke. Thus what we now write as $(x) f(x)$ was written by Frege as:

He uses Gothic letters for bound variables, and italic letters for free variables, with the convention that the scope of a free variable is the whole of the proposition in which it occurs.

The appearance of formulae on the page may be glimpsed in the single formula below, of which an instance in ordinary language would be: If all women are foolish if they are rich, then Cleopatra is foolish if she is a rich woman.

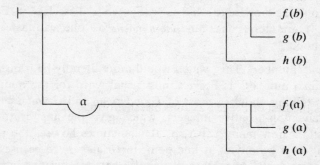

Greek letters do not appear as part of Frege's basic system, but he uses lower-case Greek letters for two purposes: (i) as part of abbreviative definitions; and (ii) to indicate the argument place in a function, as in ξ *is greater than 0*. Upper-case Greek letters are used to talk *about* the system, as for instance in stating its rules, thus:

'From the two statements '$\vdash \underset{\Delta}{\overset{\Gamma}{\llcorner}}$ and $\vdash \Delta$ ' we may derive the statement '$\vdash \Gamma$'.

A NOTE ON TRANSLATION

I list below the English renderings which I have generally used for technical terms in Frege's German. Where no comment is made, the rendering is the one generally used by translators and commentators. Where more than one English equivalent is in use, I have added a note to justify my preference.

anerkennen 'accept'. This is the mental equivalent of the speech-act of asserting. Most translators render it as 'acknowledge', but that will not do because 'acknowledge' is a success verb – one can only acknowledge what is true – while it is clear in Frege that, regrettably, one can *anerkennen*, as one can assert, a falsehood.

Anzahl 'number'. This, which would more literally be translated 'cardinal number', is Frege's most usual word for the numbers he is talking about in most of *Foundations* and *Grundgesetze* – namely, non-negative integers, which give the answer to the question 'how many?' (FA, p. 5). Sometimes he uses the word 'Zahl' as a synonym; at one point in *Grundgesetze* he uses the contrast 'Zahl'/'Anzahl' to distinguish between positive integers and real numbers. I have not followed Austin and Furth in using 'Number' for 'Anzahl', and 'number' for 'Zahl'.

ausdrücken 'express'.

Aussage 'statement'. 'Assertion' is also possible, but I have avoided it to prevent confusion with the act of asserting.

bedeuten 'signify', 'stand for', 'refer to'.

Bedeutung 'reference'. Prior to *Function and Concept* the word is used in the general sense of 'meaning' or 'signification' and I have thus translated it. Once it has been introduced as a technical term to contrast with *Sinn* I have used 'reference', preferring it to 'meaning', which invites confusion, and to 'denotation', which is far less common in the general literature of the topic.

Begriff 'concept'.

begriffliche Inhalt 'conceptual content'.

Begriffschrift 'concept script'. I have used this (in preference to 'ideography' or 'conceptual notation') both as a generic term and as a title for Frege's pamphlet.

Behauptung 'assertion'.

Gedanke 'thought'.

Gegenstand 'object'.

gleich 'alike'. The German word can mean either 'identical', 'equal' or 'alike'. Sometimes Frege's text reads more convincingly if we translate it as 'identical' or sometimes if we translate it as 'alike'. In fact, since Frege believed that no two non-identical things were totally alike, the ambiguity is not important. See p. 71.

Gleichheit 'identity', 'equation'.

gleichzahlig 'equivalent'. The word is a coinage of Frege's, and its meaning is given by his explanation (see p. 89). Other translators use 'like-numbered', which is too literal, 'equal', which does not sound technical enough, or 'equinumerous', which is too ugly.

Inhalt 'content'.

Merkmal 'component' (of a concept). The literal translation is 'characteristic', but this clashes with the explanation which Frege gives, which is that a *merkmal* is an item which helps to put together a concept. A *Merkmal* is a characteristic not of the concept, but of the objects falling under the concept.

Satz 'proposition'. The German word, in Frege, commonly means a sentence with a sense. The English word 'proposition' can mean this, or it can mean an abstract object expressed by such a sentence, which is what Frege calls a 'thought'. In some of Frege's later writings, the word is used in such a way that 'sentence' is the more natural translation, and I have rendered the word accordingly.

Sinn 'sense'.

Umfang 'extension'.

Urteil 'judgement'.

Vorstellung 'image'. The word is often used by Kant, and in his works is commonly translated as 'representation' or 'idea'. Frege most commonly uses it to mean a mental image. In his later writings he sometimes uses it in a broader sense to include, for example, sense impressions. In that context I translate it by 'idea'.

Wertverlauf 'value-range'. The translation 'course of values' is clumsy, and the danger of confusion with other senses of 'range' is slight. Obviously it does not mean class of possible values of a function.

wirklich '(causally) active'. 'Actual' is the translation preferred by most writers, but that word contains irrelevant suggestions of the contrast between actual and potential, or actual and defunct. *Wirklichkeit* is the world of causal interaction, the workaday world. Numbers, for Frege, are objective, and real, but they are not active.

INDEX

INDEX

READ MORE IN PENGUIN

In every corner of the world, on every subject under the sun, Penguin represents quality and variety – the very best in publishing today.

For complete information about books available from Penguin – including Puffins, Penguin Classics and Arkana – and how to order them, write to us at the appropriate address below. Please note that for copyright reasons the selection of books varies from country to country.

In the United Kingdom: Please write to *Dept. EP, Penguin Books Ltd, Bath Road, Harmondsworth, West Drayton, Middlesex UB7 0DA*

In the United States: Please write to *Consumer Sales, Penguin USA, P.O. Box 999, Dept. 17109, Bergenfield, New Jersey 07621-0120.* VISA and MasterCard holders call 1-800-253-6476 to order Penguin titles

In Canada: Please write to *Penguin Books Canada Ltd, 10 Alcorn Avenue, Suite 300, Toronto, Ontario M4V 3B2*

In Australia: Please write to *Penguin Books Australia Ltd, P.O. Box 257, Ringwood, Victoria 3134*

In New Zealand: Please write to *Penguin Books (NZ) Ltd, Private Bag 102902, North Shore Mail Centre, Auckland 10*

In India: Please write to *Penguin Books India Pvt Ltd, 706 Eros Apartments, 56 Nehru Place, New Delhi 110 019*

In the Netherlands: Please write to *Penguin Books Netherlands bv, Postbus 3507, NL-1001 AH Amsterdam*

In Germany: Please write to *Penguin Books Deutschland GmbH, Metzlerstrasse 26, 60594 Frankfurt am Main*

In Spain: Please write to *Penguin Books S. A., Bravo Murillo 19, 1° B, 28015 Madrid*

In Italy: Please write to *Penguin Italia s.r.l., Via Felice Casati 20, I–20124 Milano*

In France: Please write to *Penguin France S. A., 17 rue Lejeune, F–31000 Toulouse*

In Japan: Please write to *Penguin Books Japan, Ishikiribashi Building, 2–5–4, Suido, Bunkyo-ku, Tokyo 112*

In South Africa: Please write to *Longman Penguin Southern Africa (Pty) Ltd, Private Bag X08, Bertsham 2013*

READ MORE IN PENGUIN

SCIENCE AND MATHEMATICS

The Character of Physical Law   Richard P. Feynman

'Richard Feynman had both genius and highly unconventional style . . .
His contributions touched almost every corner of the subject, and have had
a deep and abiding influence over the way that physicists think' – Paul
Davies

A Mathematician Reads the Newspapers   John Allen Paulos

In this book, John Allen Paulos continues his liberating campaign against
mathematical illiteracy. 'Mathematics is all around you. And it's a great
defence against the sharks, cowboys and liars who want your vote, your
money or your life' – Ian Stewart

Bully for Brontosaurus   Stephen Jay Gould

'He fossicks through history, here and there picking up a bone, an imprint,
a fossil dropping, and, from these, tries to reconstruct the past afresh in all
its messy ambiguity. It's the droppings that provide the freshness: he's as
likely to quote from Mark Twain or Joe DiMaggio as from Lamarck or
Lavoisier' – *Guardian*

Are We Alone?   Paul Davies

Since ancient times people have been fascinated by the idea of
extraterrestrial life; today we are searching systematically for it. Paul
Davies's striking new book examines the assumptions that go into this
search and draws out the startling implications for science, religion and our
world view, should we discover that we are not alone.

The Making of the Atomic Bomb   Richard Rhodes

'Rhodes handles his rich trove of material with the skill of a master
novelist . . . his portraits of the leading figures are three-dimensional and
penetrating . . . the sheer momentum of the narrative is breathtaking . . . a
book to read and to read again' – *Guardian*

READ MORE IN PENGUIN

PHILOSOPHY

Values of Art Malcolm Budd

'Budd is a first-rate thinker . . . He brings to aesthetics formidable gifts of precision, far-sightedness and argument, together with a wide philosophical knowledge and a sincere belief in the importance of art' – *The Times*

Montaigne and Melancholy M. A. Screech

'A sensitive probe into how Montaigne resolved for himself the age-old ambiguities of melancholia and, in doing so, spoke of what he called the "human condition"' – *London Review of Books*

Labyrinths of Reason William Poundstone

'The world and what is in it, even what people say to you, will not seem the same after plunging into *Labyrinths of Reason* . . . He holds up the deepest philosophical questions for scrutiny and examines their relation to reality in a way that irresistibly sweeps readers on' – *New Scientist*

Metaphysics as a Guide to Morals Iris Murdoch

'This is philosophy dragged from the cloister, dusted down and made freshly relevant to suffering and egoism, death and religious ecstasy . . . and how we feel compassion for others' – *Guardian*

The Penguin Dictionary of Philosophy Edited by Thomas Mautner

This new dictionary encompasses all aspects of Western philosophy from 600 BC to the present day. With contributions from over a hundred leading philosophers, and including cross-references and unique usage notes, this dictionary will prove the ideal reference for any student or teacher of philosophy as well as for all those with a general interest in the subject.

Russian Thinkers Isaiah Berlin

As one of the most outstanding liberal intellects of this century, the author brings to his portraits of Russian thinkers a unique perception of the social and political circumstances that produced men such as Herzen, Bakunin, Turgenev, Belinsky and Tolstoy.

Wittgenstein

A clear and concise account of the whole range of Wittgenstein's work in the philosophy of language and the philosophy of the mind.

'Dr Kenny lays out the main elements, exposing apparent conflicts and misfits, and then, by dint of some deft shuffling of the pieces, suddenly reveals an interpretation of Wittgenstein's work that reconciles its apparently disparate elements. His achievement is an account of Wittgenstein's philosophical development that yields a persuasive picture, with minimum force, maximum ingenuity and admirable clarity' – *The Times Literary Supplement*